THE EVOLUTION OF Birds

by Carol Hand

Content Consultant

Frederick E. Wasserman
Associate Professor
Biology
Boston University

Essential Library
An Imprint of Abdo Publishing | abdobooks.com

ANIMAL EVOLUTION

abdobooks.com

Published by Abdo Publishing, a division of ABDO, PO Box 398166, Minneapolis, Minnesota 55439.

Printed in the United States of America, North Mankato, Minnesota.
082018
012019

Cover Photo: Steve Byland/Shutterstock Images
Interior Photos: Julius T. Csotonyi/Science Source, 4–5; Mehau Kulyk/Science Source, 7; José Antonio Peñas/Science Source, 10; Mikkel Juul Jensen/Science Source, 13; Shutterstock Images, 17 (chart), 23, 26, 33, 54–55, 79; Alsu Gizzatullina/Shutterstock Images, 17 (blue jay); Ben Den Hartog/iStockphoto, 18; iStockphoto, 30, 44, 74, 80, 82–83, 86; Phil Degginger/Science Source, 35; Melinda Fawver/Shutterstock Images, 36–37; Keith Pritchard/Shutterstock Images, 38; Ondrej Prosicky/Shutterstock Images, 40; Prasit Chansareekorn/iStockphoto, 46–47; Claude Huot/Shutterstock Images, 51; Natacha Pisarenko/AP Images, 57; Mircea Costina/Shutterstock, 58; Gilbert S. Grant/Science Source, 60; Michal Pesata/Shutterstock Images, 61; Ken Canning/iStockphoto, 62–63; Jaime Chirinos/Science Source, 66; Andrew M. Allport/Shutterstock Images, 68; Lori Labrecque/Shutterstock Images, 70; On the Wing Photography/Shutterstock Images, 72–73; Photoshot/Newscom, 77; Phil Degginger/Carnegie Museum/Science Source, 90–91; Pascal Goetgheluck/Science Source, 95; Martin Shields/Science Source, 99

Editor: Marie Pearson
Series Designer: Becky Daum

Library of Congress Control Number: 2018947966

Publisher's Cataloging-in-Publication Data

Names: Hand, Carol, author.
Title: The evolution of birds / by Carol Hand.
Description: Minneapolis, Minnesota : Abdo Publishing, 2019 | Series: Animal evolution | Includes online resources and index.
Identifiers: ISBN 9781532116636 (lib. bdg.) | ISBN 9781532159473 (ebook)
Subjects: LCSH: Birds--Evolution--Juvenile literature. | Animal evolution--Juvenile literature. | Biological evolution--Juvenile literature. | Birds--Juvenile literature.
Classification: DDC 574.30--dc23

CONTENTS

CHAPTER ONE

From *T. Rex* to Turkeys

It is approximately 160 million years ago (MYA) in the late Jurassic period (201.3–145 MYA). In a forest in the northeastern part of what is now China, a long-tailed, chicken-sized animal clings to a tree trunk and scrambles its way upward. Its fingers and toes end in claws, which are great for climbing, but when it reaches a branch, it cannot perch. Its toe structure is not developed for perching. Instead, it clings to the branch with its claws. When it gets tired of the treetops, it extends its arms and legs and glides to the ground. The rows of feathers along the length of both its arms and legs form something like four wings.

Anchiornis may have fed on insects.

The animal's feathers are not like those of modern birds, which have vanes of barbs that zip together and extend from a central shaft. Instead, they have vanes consisting of short, flexible barbs that don't easily stick together. This mass of feathers gives the animal a fluffy, scruffy appearance. These feathers are not very efficient for flight. Although they help with insulation and repel water, they aren't great at those jobs either. This little animal, with its four feathered wings, is a dinosaur called *Anchiornis*. Although not yet a bird, it is well on its way to becoming one.

Paleontologists discovered the first *Anchiornis* fossils in China in 2009. Since then, more than 200 similar fossils have been found. One group of scientists has pieced together descriptions of *Anchiornis*'s structure and movement. Others have used a technique

A BIRD LIKE A DINOSAUR

Hoatzins don't fit in with other birds. According to *Audubon* writer Elizabeth Deatrick, these scruffy Amazon jungle birds "never got the genetic message that they aren't dinosaurs anymore."[1] For one thing, their chicks have claws just like *Anchiornis*'s. Hoatzins build nests on branches overhanging the water. When predators such as snakes appear, chicks drop from the nest into the safety of the water. They swim to land after the snake leaves, then use their claws to climb the tree and return to the nest. The hoatzin's claws disappear in adulthood, but it remains a clumsy flier for its entire life. A 2014 DNA study indicated the hoatzin is most closely related to shorebirds such as cranes and plovers—but not very closely related. It branched off from other birds approximately 65 MYA.

Archaeopteryx lithographica was the size of a large crow.

called laser-stimulated fluorescence to look at the fossils. In the fluorescence technique, a laser is pointed at the fossil in a dark room and scientists record the wavelengths of light that bounce off. This helped scientists determine *Anchiornis*'s feather coloration: a black-and-gray body, white highlights, and a red crest.

ARCHAEOPTERYX

The first fossil skeleton to give a clue about bird origins was uncovered in 1861 in southern Germany. The bird, named *Archaeopteryx lithographica*, lived approximately 150 MYA, when

Germany was an archipelago with a Florida-like climate. Because it had characteristics of both birds and reptiles, *A. lithographica* was considered a transitional fossil that linked dinosaurs with modern birds.

Eleven more *A. lithographica* fossils have since been found in Germany. The bird was raven sized, weighing approximately two pounds (1 kg). It had broad, rounded wings and a tail up to 20 inches (50 cm) long.[2] Fluffy feathers covered its body and legs. Scientists aren't sure if it had head or neck feathers.

In 2018, an international group of scientists using state-of-the-art technology at a facility in France tried to understand the flying abilities of *A. lithographica*. Using synchrotron microtomography, a type of X-ray imaging, the scientists were able to create a three-dimensional (3-D) image that allowed them to see inside the fossilized bones without damaging them. They discovered that

DINOSAURS ARE NOT EXTINCT

Dr. Christopher Eppig says that when people eat chicken or turkey, they are eating dinosaurs. Birds are not simply similar to dinosaurs, he says. They are not merely related to dinosaurs. They actually are dinosaurs.

Since the mid-1990s, evidence for birds' dinosaur origins has grown. Pieces of this evidence have included shared skeletal features and the discovery of dinosaur feathers. According to the Understanding Evolution website at University of California, Berkeley, "Birds are simply a twig on the dinosaurs' branch of the tree of life."[3]

A. lithographica's wing bones were much thinner than those of ground-dwelling dinosaurs. They were actually very similar to modern pheasant bones. Pheasants are not strong fliers. They use short flights to evade predators or cross barriers.

THEROPODS GIVE RISE TO BIRDS

There are two theories about how flight evolved. In one theory, a tree-dwelling ancestor began by gliding to the ground. It could remain in the air longer when it flapped its forelimbs. A second theory suggests that a small, ground-dwelling ancestor ran on two legs and extended its forelimbs as it leaped to catch prey or avoid predators. Feathers would have improved lift, making flight easier.

Fossils help scientists find more answers about the origins and evolution of flight. Birds have a very limited fossil record because their thin, lightweight bones tend to disintegrate rather than form fossils. Paleontologists piece together the bones that have survived, providing a clearer picture of bird origins.

Scientists found the first *A. lithographica* fossil just after the 1859 publication of Charles Darwin's *On the Origin of Species*. But *A. lithographica* was not the origin of modern birds. True birds probably arose from the end of the Triassic (251.9–201.3 MYA) to the beginning of

Velociraptor had feathers.

the Jurassic periods, but their ancestors likely began to diverge, or become different, from dinosaurs anywhere from 227 to 174 MYA. These ancestors were probably a group of theropod dinosaurs called coelurosaurs. Theropods, which include *Tyrannosaurus rex* and *Velociraptor*, were carnivorous and bipedal (meaning two footed), which freed the front limbs for other uses, including flight.

Coelurosaurs probably began decreasing in size approximately 200 MYA, about 50 million years before *A. lithographica* appeared. Small size was probably essential for flight. A series of morphological, or physical, changes followed as theropods evolved into birds. First, long bones became hollow, and the first foot digit lost its role in supporting weight. Second, the function of grasping hands improved with the evolution of a rotating wrist joint. Third, the coracoid bone of the shoulder and the sternum, or breastbone, expanded, which helped support bigger, stronger muscles and more feathers. Fourth, vaned feathers appeared, arranged by precise types and layers. Fifth, the trunk shortened and the tail became stiffer, which improved balance and maneuverability. Sixth, changes in the shoulder joint, the development of a wing and asymmetrical feathers, and the reversal of the inner toe supported basic flight and perching.

These changes all occurred very early in bird evolution. The sixth group of changes appears in *A. lithographica*. Further refinements of physical structures lending themselves to powered flight and perching followed. Beginning approximately 150 MYA, the thorax, or chest, became deeper. Bones of the shoulder and pelvis became strut shaped for better support. Then new adaptations formed, including a tendon for wing-muscle attachment, feathers to control airflow, fan-shaped tail feathers, and a fully opposable inner toe for perching. Next, the shoulder blades fused to form the wishbone. A deep ridge called a keel extended from the breastbone, enabling huge chest muscles to develop, which are essential for powered flight.

All of these adaptations were in place during the Cretaceous period (145–66 MYA), but the explosion in bird diversity didn't begin until the end of that period, shortly after an asteroid strike caused the extinction of the larger dinosaurs. The few survivors of the asteroid served as the basis for the thousands of bird species to come. For example, a fossil of *Vegavis iaai*, found in Antarctica in 2005, was dated to 67 MYA, just before the asteroid hit Earth. Very similar to the modern-day duck, *V. iaai* is considered to be part of today's line of birds.

Feathers

It's logical to assume that modern bird feathers evolved for flight. But feathers existed long before flight. Many dinosaurs had feathers. They probably first served as insulation, which is vital for temperature regulation in warm-blooded animals. Later, some dinosaurs developed long feathers on their arms and legs. An oviraptorosaur fossil from China's Gobi Desert was found hunched over a nest of eggs with its feathered arms spread over them. Many dinosaurs may have had feathers with colors and patterns. A 160-million-year-old *Epidexipteryx* fossil had long, ribbonlike feathers that its Chinese discoverers think were used in mating displays.

Scientists think feathers evolved in five stages. In stage one, an unbranched, hollow filament developed from a cavity surrounding a small bump in the epidermis, or outer skin layer. In stage two, several filaments fused at their bases, forming a tuft. Stage three occurred in two parts. In part A, a rachis, or central branch, developed, with a series of fused barbs along its length. In part B, secondary barbs called barbules formed at right angles from the barbs. Stages four and five represent more modern feathers. In stage four, the vane, or main part, of the feather closed as the barbs and barbules hooked together. In stage five, the feather became asymmetrical; that is, the rachis was no longer central, but skewed to one side. This makes the feather much more efficient for flight.

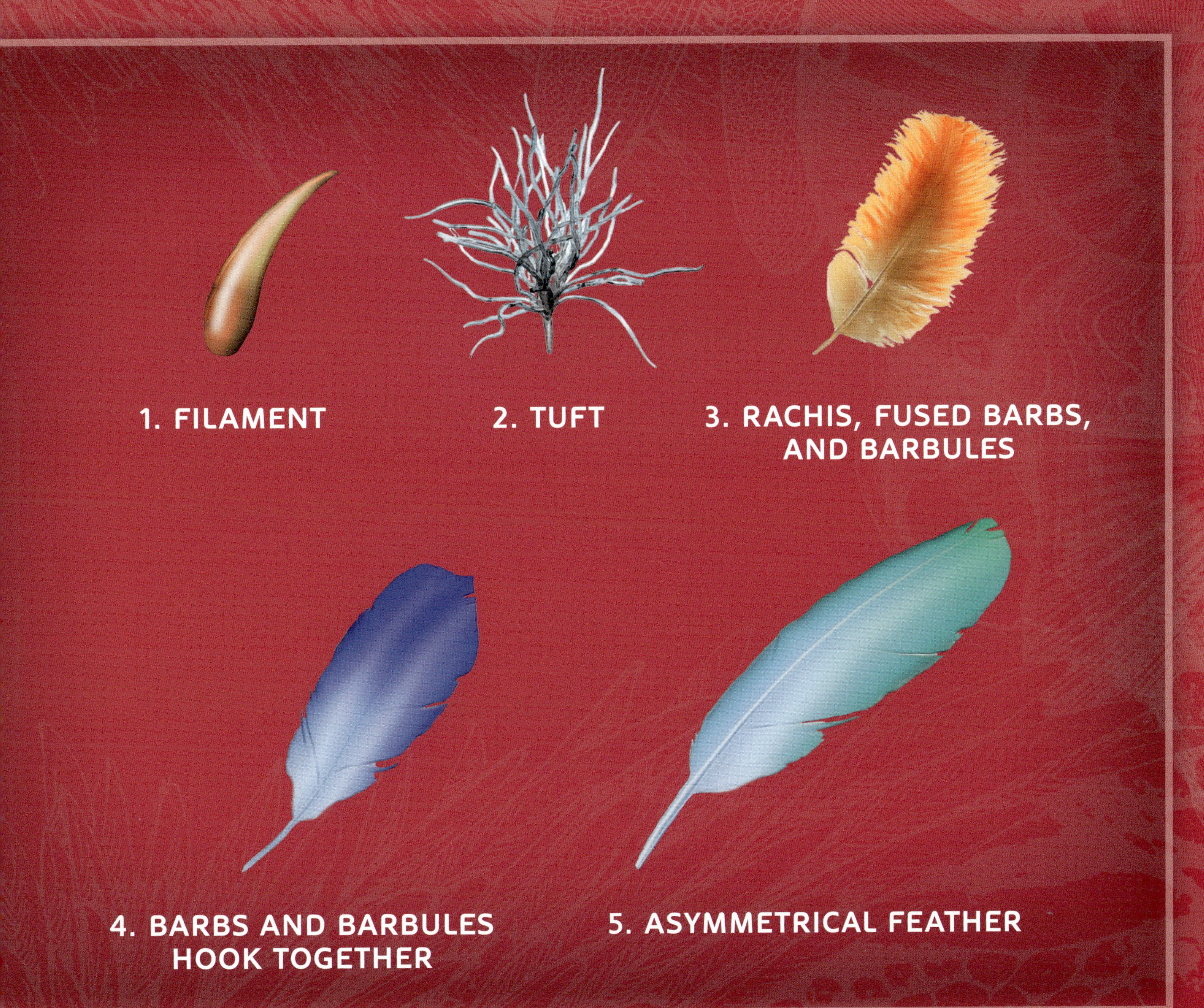
1. FILAMENT
2. TUFT
3. RACHIS, FUSED BARBS, AND BARBULES
4. BARBS AND BARBULES HOOK TOGETHER
5. ASYMMETRICAL FEATHER

HOW EVOLUTION WORKS

Evolution is descent with modification. This description recognizes that all organisms have a common ancestor and that all changes occurring through generations represent genetic modifications from that ancestor. Genetics helps explain how evolution works. An organism's genome, or complete set of genes, is basically a recipe for making that organism. Genes control what proteins an organism produces. These proteins determine the organism's structure, physiology, and behavior. As a gene changes within a population, the protein, and therefore the characteristic that gene controls, also changes.

Evolution requires genetic variation. In other words, members of a population must have variations in a trait. For example, a population may include individuals with brown, blue, or

BIRDS AND CROCODILES

Comparisons of the genomes of 45 newly analyzed bird species led scientists to rearrange some branches of the bird evolutionary tree.[4] Down near the root of the bird tree is a fierce group of ancestors, the archosaurs. The name *archosaur* means "ruling reptile." It lived approximately 250 MYA. This ancestor split into two main groups. One group formed crocodiles and their kin, which have changed little over the millennia. The other group evolved rapidly into various groups of dinosaurs, one of which eventually became birds.

green eyes. Evolution also requires selective pressure, or a push to change resulting from a stressful environmental factor. Factors such as drought or new predators might cause selective pressure. When genetic variation meets selective pressure, some individuals are better suited than others to survive and reproduce. For instance, faster runners might better survive a new predator. Over time, the proportion of a genetic trait increases or decreases in the population, resulting in changes in the population's overall appearance, behavior, or physiology.

A group of birds on the Galápagos Islands known as Darwin's finches provides a clear example of evolution. In 1977, a severe drought killed off many medium ground finches on the island of Daphne Major. Large seeds became much more plentiful than small ones, and the finches with larger beaks were better able to crack the large seeds. Over the following years, finches with larger beaks survived better than those with smaller ones. The average beak size of the island's finches increased. This is an example of food-influenced natural selection.

BIRDS TODAY

Birds are members of the kingdom Animalia. That means they're animals. They are members of the phylum Chordata, which includes all animals with backbones in a subphylum called Vertebrata. The seven classes of vertebrates include amphibians, reptiles, birds, mammals, and three groups of fishes. These classifications are based primarily on the animals' skeletal systems, reproductive systems, and environmental adaptations. Birds, or class Aves, produce eggs that are protected by a shell and membranes. They are warm blooded, or able to maintain their body temperatures. They have wings and feathers.

This system of classification is useful for understanding how animals live in the environment. But as the study of evolution has progressed, scientists have developed new classifications based on evolutionary relationships. These phylogenetic classifications show birds as part of the branch of reptiles, which is part of the dinosaur family tree. Both types of classifications are useful, and both are used in different situations.

No one knows for sure how many bird species there are, but the number exceeds 10,000. Although scientific understanding of bird lineages shifts as ornithologists learn more about their evolution, the modern class Aves includes as many as 40 orders.[5] Separate orders cover types such as birds of prey, hummingbirds, owls, parrots, and perching birds. Birds are incredibly diverse, and although people have studied them for centuries, their secrets are still being uncovered.

CLASSIFICATION

Blue Jay
Cyanocitta cristata

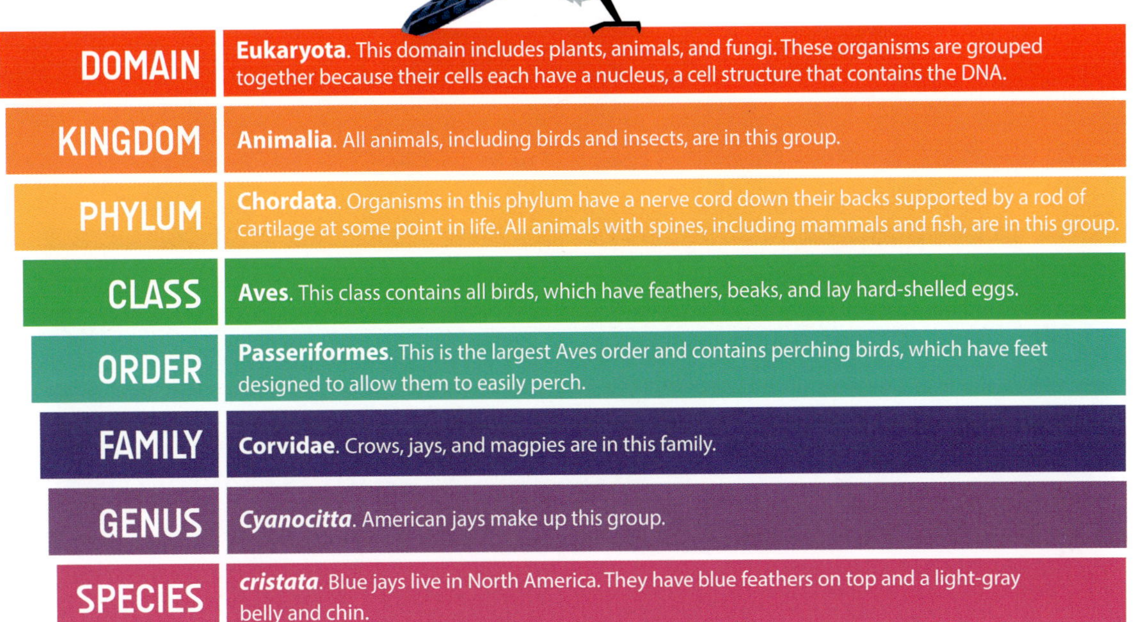

Taxonomic classification is the science of identifying living things, grouping them together, and naming them. When this is done, each organism is assigned a place in eight different categories ranging from domain, the most general category, to species, the most specific category. When the scientific name of an animal is given, it includes the genus, which is capitalized, and the species, which is not. Blue jays are *Cyanocitta cristata*. Scientific names are often abbreviated after first use: *C. cristata*.

CHAPTER TWO

Flightless Birds

Birds are usually pictured as relatively small and feathered flying animals. But there are also huge flightless birds. These birds, called ratites, are members of the bird order Struthioniformes. They include the ostrich, emu, cassowary, and rhea, plus the now-extinct moa and elephant bird. There are smaller ratites, too, such as the chicken-sized kiwi and the tinamou. The smallest ratite is the dwarf tinamou, which weighs just 1.5 ounces (42 g).[1] The largest living ratite, the ostrich, can reach a height of nine feet (2.7 m) and weigh 320 pounds (145 kg).[2] The extinct birds were even larger. The elephant bird reached 10 feet (3 m) in height and the moa was nearly as large.[3]

Ratites are flightless. Their breastbones lack a keel, which is the large ridge to which flight muscles attach. Also, their wings are small and weak compared to their large bodies and long legs. Ratites inhabit different continents and islands in the Southern Hemisphere. Ostriches are

Scientists do not yet understand the purpose of the casque, or helmet, on the top of a cassowary's head.

FLIGHTLESS NON-RATITES

Two flightless non-ratites are the flightless cormorant, also called the Galápagos cormorant, and the now-extinct dodo bird. These birds provide insights into the environmental conditions that cause birds to become flightless. Both evolved on islands. With few or no land predators, they had less need for flight to escape. Natural selection favored swimming to obtain fish as food.

There are 29 species of cormorants, which are large diving seabirds classified in the same order as pelicans.[4] Found only on two of the Galápagos Islands, flightless cormorants are the only members of the cormorant family that cannot fly. That's because their wings, which spread for balance when they hop from rock to rock, are one-third of the length needed for flight. A 2017 study of the flightless cormorant's genetics identified four genes relating to limb formation that are nonfunctional in this species but highly active in other bird groups. This accounts for the flightless cormorant's reduced wing size and lack of other skeletal features necessary for flight.

found in Africa, rheas and tinamous in South America, emus and cassowaries in Australia, and kiwis and the extinct moa in New Zealand. The extinct elephant bird lived on Madagascar, off the coast of Africa.

OLD IDEAS ABOUT RATITE EVOLUTION

In 1839, British biologist Richard Owen identified the first fossil of the extinct moa as a giant bird. Darwin, also working in the 1800s, noticed similarities in flightless birds around the world. He assumed they must be related. Darwin's contemporary, Thomas Huxley, had observed that bones in the ratite palate, or roof of the mouth, are more reptilelike in arrangement than those of other birds. This suggested a close relationship between ratite species.

Scientists have proposed two major hypotheses for how single species or populations diversify into new species: vicariance and dispersal. In vicariance, an existing population is fragmented into two or more parts because of a new barrier, such as a mountain range or ocean. In dispersal, the existing population moves across an existing barrier. In both cases, the separation of groups leads to differentiation and eventually speciation (the development of new species that can no longer interbreed with the ancestral species).

Since Darwin's time, scientists have debated the origin of ratite species. Originally, because the birds were similar, they assumed ratites evolved as one large group. This would have begun approximately 200 MYA, when Earth's landmass had only two huge continents. They assumed the single ratite ancestor, a flightless bird, lived on Gondwana, the southern of the two continents. As the landmass separated to form modern-day continents, groups of ancestor birds would have been isolated onto separate continents and begun to diversify. According to this hypothesis, vicariance explained the separation of ancestral ratites and how all of today's ratite groups came from a common flightless ancestor.

DNA ANALYSIS CLEARS UP RELATIONSHIPS

Today's scientists can better understand relationships among ratites by comparing their DNA. Similarities between two species' DNA sequences, or the order of the base pairs connecting the two DNA strands, indicate the species are very closely related. Base pairs are made of two nucleotides, which are building blocks of DNA. Scientists made such comparisons in 2014 by studying 1,500 DNA segments from various types of ratites.[5]

The tinamou has been particularly difficult to classify. It has a keeled breastbone and can fly, although not well, suggesting it evolved with flying birds. But its palate bones match those of ratites. Based on these conflicting features, scientists tentatively decided tinamous were related, though not closely, to ratites. But DNA analyses placed tinamous squarely within the

GONDWANA

Earth's continents were once combined into a single supercontinent called Pangaea. Approximately 200 MYA, Pangaea began to separate into two continents: Laurasia in the north and Gondwana in the south. This was during the Jurassic, when Earth was very warm. Much of Gondwana was covered in rain forest, and there was no Antarctic ice sheet. Gondwana itself began to break apart approximately 170 to 180 MYA. The gradual movement of continents, called continental drift, eventually resulted in today's southern landmasses: Africa, South America, Australia, Antarctica, the Indian subcontinent, and the Arabian Peninsula.

The elegant crested tinamou feeds on many things, including seeds, leaves, and insects.

middle of the ratite group. They show a close relationship with the giant extinct moa, native to New Zealand until humans wiped it out 12,000 years ago.

Another team, with lead author Kieren Mitchell, studied DNA that same year. They found that size is no predictor of relationships. DNA sequences from extinct elephant birds showed that these giants are most closely related to today's chicken-sized kiwi. The two arose from a common ancestor some 50 MYA, after New Zealand had become isolated. Scientists expected elephant birds to be more closely related to ostriches, which they resemble. But DNA comparisons show ostriches and elephant birds are only distantly related.

THE ELEPHANT BIRD

The elephant bird, of the genus *Aepyornis*, evolved on the island of Madagascar, a land of lush tropical vegetation and few predators. *Aepyornis* had the same body type as birdlike dinosaurs such as *Deinocheirus*, which were fully formed 70 MYA and weighed seven short tons (6 metric tons). Unlike *Deinocheirus*, *Aepyornis* was not as big as an elephant, but it was huge—Earth's largest bird ever. It reached ten feet (3 m) in height and weighed 605 pounds (275 kg). Its closest living relative is the 11-pound (5 kg) kiwi. Scientists have found fossil elephant-bird eggs. Scientists think a small population of kiwi-like birds flew to Madagascar millions of years ago and eventually evolved into elephant birds. According to Mitchell, the close relationship between the kiwi and the elephant bird "highlights the power of evolution to produce radically different forms over a relatively short period of time."[6]

ORIGINS OF RATITES

In 2014, a team of scientists studied genetic data of two elephant bird species. Mitchell noted the study led to a completely new view of ratite origins. The team's research suggests ratites did not evolve from a single flightless ancestor when members of that species became isolated on newly formed continents. Instead, their ancestors apparently flew long distances to different regions of the world, where each group evolved to become flightless. Their speciation was based on dispersal rather than vicariance.

Flightless birds evolved to lose the flight abilities of their ancestors, and each group became flightless independently.

Mitchell believes the ratite ancestor may have been a lithornithid, a now-extinct group similar to tinamous and approximately the size of a quail or chicken. Members of the species probably dispersed to points around the world approximately 65 MYA, around the same time large dinosaurs were dying out and ecological niches were developing around the world. Lithornithids were apparently highly mobile. Their fossils have been found in both Europe and North America, even though ratites are not found on these continents.

In other words, all ratites did evolve from a common ancestor. However, that ancestor was likely a flying bird that flew to every continent. Groups of ratite ancestors were not already on each continent as the continents moved away from each other.

CHAPTER THREE

Pigeons and Doves

All 310 species of pigeons and doves belong to the order Columbiformes. They are found around the world except in extremely hot or cold locations. People use the terms *pigeon* and *dove* interchangeably, but ornithologists usually call the larger species pigeons and the smaller ones doves. Commonly, the term *pigeon* is used when referencing sports, hobbies, or food. *Dove* has a more religious connotation.

Pigeons and doves have a stout body type with short necks and legs. Their beaks are short and slender with fleshy ceres, or coverings, at the base that contain the nostrils. These birds are gentle, intelligent, and, in some cases, easy to domesticate. In the wild, they gather in large flocks. Most people are familiar with the flocks found in cities, which are often considered nuisances. This species is variously known as the feral rock pigeon, city pigeon, or rock dove.

Crowned pigeons are the largest pigeons, weighing up to 8.8 pounds (4 kg).

THE PASSENGER PIGEON

In May 1850, Simon Pokagon, a Potawatomi leader, described the arrival of a flock of passenger pigeons: "While I gazed in wonder and astonishment, I beheld moving toward me in an unbroken front millions of pigeons." Passenger pigeons were then the most abundant bird in North America. Their migrating flocks took hours to pass over a single spot. Fifty years later, they were nearly gone.[1] The passenger pigeon has become a symbol of rapid extinction caused by humans. Early settlers shrank these birds' habitats by cutting down forests. They were always hunted as food, but professional hunters began killing them by the thousands and sold them to city markets. Passenger pigeons lived in social groups and required large numbers to reproduce successfully. As their numbers declined, they were unable to breed or raise young, so they quickly died out. Martha, the last passenger pigeon, died on September 1, 1914, in the Cincinnati Zoo. She was 29 years old.

PIGEON ORIGINS AND HOMING ABILITY

Most modern bird orders, including pigeons and doves, existed in their current form by 35 MYA during the late part of the Paleogene period (66–23 MYA). But very few bird fossils of any kind have been found from the Cretaceous, when birds were likely diversifying. There may have been few birds during that time, or the fragile bird bones simply did not preserve well. Pigeons and doves are not well represented in the fossil record, so little is known about their ancestors or how they evolved. Fossil fragments from a fruit pigeon, aged 16 to 19 million years, found in New Zealand in 2009, indicated pigeons had already evolved into their modern form. The oldest-known passenger pigeon fossil—a single wing bone—was found in 2001 in North Carolina. Tests showed it to be 3.7 to 4.8 million years old.

Though the origins of the pigeon are murky, the evolution of one of its traits has made it valuable to humans for thousands of years. As long ago as ancient Phoenician times (1500–332 BCE), humans have relied on pigeons for their navigation skills. According to biologist Hans G. Wallraff, pigeon navigation involves both a map and a compass. The map tells them where home is, and the compass tells them how to get there.

Scientists do not yet fully understand the pigeon's map. Some think it's magnetic, which would allow them to use Earth's magnetic fields as a means of navigation. Other scientists think pigeons use infrasound, or sound below human hearing. Still others think that pigeons use their sense of smell to navigate. Regardless of how, pigeons sense the location of their home roost. When released south of their home location, they recognize "south" and therefore fly north to reach home.

Experience with using these internal maps actually changes pigeons' brains, specifically the hippocampus and olfactory bulbs, which become enlarged. The hippocampus is involved in long-term memory and spatial navigation. The olfactory bulbs aid in the sense of smell.

DOVES IN HISTORY

Doves are often used as symbols in religion, art, and literature. In the Mediterranean and Near East during ancient times, they were symbols of the Mother Goddess. In the Old Testament of the Bible, Noah sent doves from the ark, and they returned to him. Doves in the Bible's New Testament symbolized the Holy Spirit (pictured), one of three persons in the Trinity that is God.

PIGEONS IN HUMAN HISTORY

Humans have a long history of interaction with pigeons and doves. Doves, for example, have been religious and sacrificial symbols for centuries. They were domesticated as food for millennia in Sumer (a region of ancient Babylonia), Mesopotamia in southwestern Asia, and Europe. Carrier pigeons are known for carrying messages long distances, especially during wartime. They were used from the times of the ancient Greek city-states all the way through both world wars of the 1900s. During World War I (1914–1918), British intelligence used carrier pigeons to maintain contact with resistance movements in enemy territory. They were highly effective—their arrival rate during

World War I was 95 percent.[2] Pigeons also served as bait in the sport of falconry, which involves using falcons or other birds of prey for hunting.

During the 1800s, hundreds at a time were killed in English pigeon-shooting competitions. Pigeon breeding has been an important hobby for centuries. During the 1800s, the breeding of fancy pigeons with ruffled feathers and other exaggerated characteristics became popular, captivating the interest of everyone in England from the poorest miners to Queen Victoria.

SELECTIVE BREEDING OF PIGEONS

Following his world voyage on the HMS *Beagle*, Darwin began studying pigeons in the 1850s to build evidence for his theory of natural selection. He joined London pigeon clubs and met and learned from breeders worldwide. He bred his own fancy pigeons, measured their skeletons, and recorded variations in colors and patterns, proportions, and behaviors. He observed that birds of many different breeds could reproduce successfully, which supported the view that all pigeons arose from a single ancestral species.

Darwin also compared artificial selection, or selective breeding, to natural selection. Natural selection depends on the chance pairing of random variations that result in desired characteristics. It can take just a few years or millions of years. Artificial selection depends on human breeders deliberately mating pigeons with desired characteristics. When the selected pigeons are bred, more of their offspring have the desired characteristic. These offspring are bred with others who also have the trait, and soon a new breed is formed. Artificial selection can produce visible results in a matter of weeks, depending on the species. It works the same way as natural selection, only faster. Animal breeders have been contributing to evolution for thousands of years without realizing it.

PIGEONS TODAY

Today's domestic pigeons all evolved from the rock pigeon, *Columba livia*. The species diversified as its members were bred for different functions. Large king pigeons are bred for food. Homing or racing pigeons are bred for competitive racing. They are also used at weddings and other events and kept as pets. Fancy pigeons are bred for unusual colors and feather types. They are shown at competitions and also kept as pets.

Yet in the wild, today's pigeons are considered to be a nuisance. The pigeons that congregate in flocks in cities are feral—they have escaped from captivity and gone wild, similar to feral cats or dogs. Feral pigeons are all descendants of escaped domesticated pigeons.

Some people race pigeons, releasing them from a certain location and letting them use their navigation skills to return home.

In Europe, these feral birds have crossbred extensively with wild pigeons, so very few pure *C. livia* remain.

Most of the current population of pigeons in the United States have European ancestors and are descended from released domesticated birds. They are extremely successful and adaptable. City skyscrapers take the place of rocky ledges and cliffs that are their natural nesting areas. Pigeons prefer to nest near people, most likely because of their previous domestication. Though many people may not appreciate pigeons as much as they appreciate cats or dogs, the same type of selective breeding prominent in house pets has also made pigeons a part of human civilization.

Skeleton and Wings

Theropod dinosaurs, which eventually gave way to birds, had lost two hand digits by approximately 220 MYA. Scientists have disagreed about which digits disappeared and which led to wing formation, causing controversy about whether birds actually descended from dinosaurs. In bird fossils, wings arose from digits one, two, and three (thumb, forefinger, and middle finger). But in modern bird embryos, wings arise from digits two, three, and four. Most scientists still believe that theropod dinosaurs evolved into birds, but a few think birds and theropods had an earlier common ancestor. Regardless of which digits formed wings, the wristbones below digits one and two eventually fused and became more semicircular. This enabled the hand to rotate sideways, which eventually resulted in the wing-joint movements required for creating thrust for flight.

As dinosaurs evolved into birds, their skeletons also became much lighter. By 230 MYA, bird bones had thinned and become hollow. This made birds lighter. Bones in birds' hands, feet, shoulders, and pelvises fused. Fusion decreased the number of joints, which strengthened and stiffened the skeleton. The collarbones also fused, forming the wishbone. The breastbone developed a keel to which large flight muscles could attach.

Bird skulls also became lightweight. By 100 MYA, bird ancestors lost all teeth because teeth are heavy and hinder flying. As a result, the size of birds' jaws diminished. Teeth were replaced by beaks, which are now birds' main tool for pecking, cracking, piercing, and probing.

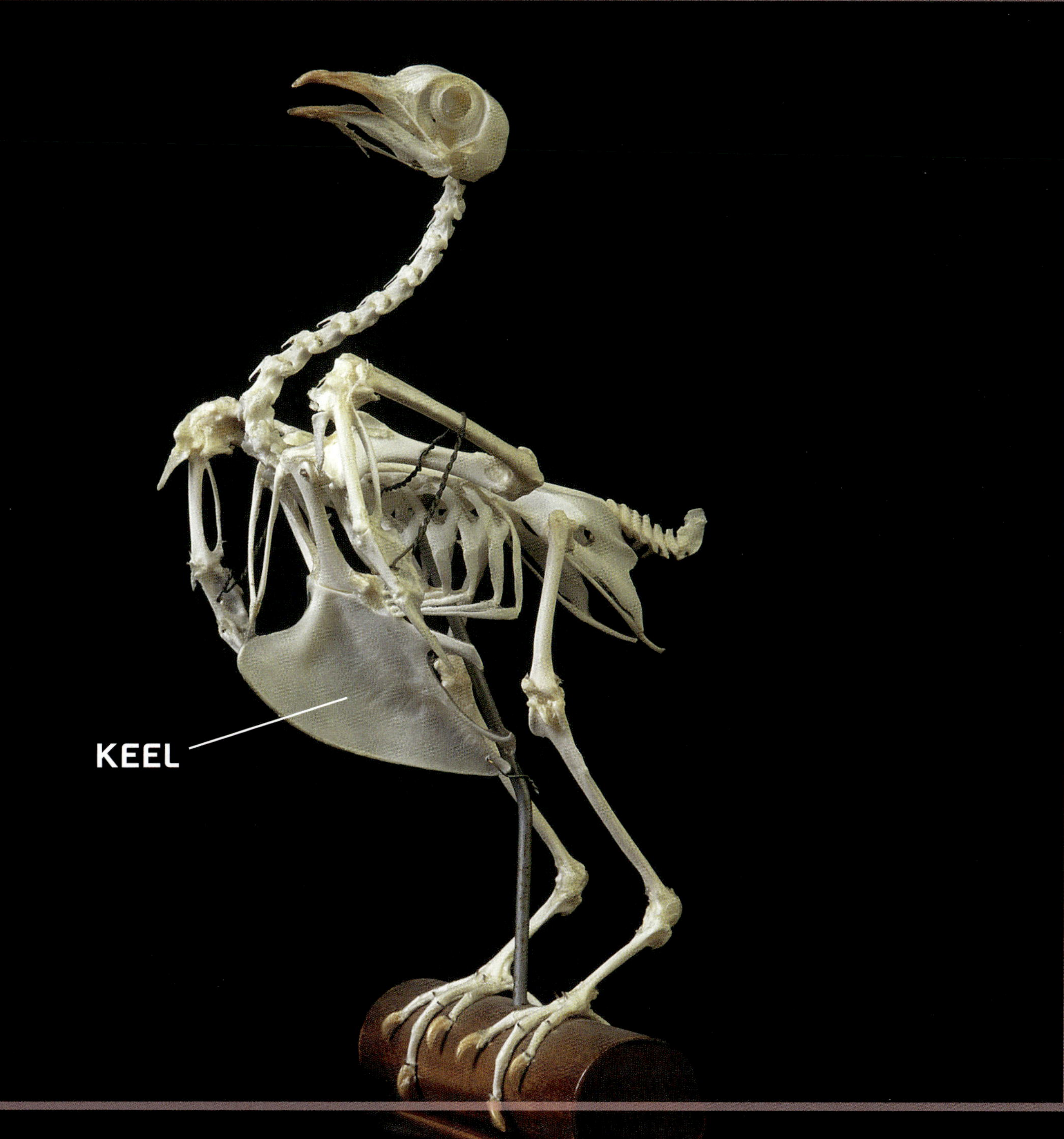
KEEL

CHAPTER FOUR

Hummingbirds

Hummingbirds are members of the order Apodiformes, meaning "footless." Hummingbird feet are tiny and used only for perching. The birds cannot walk or hop. When hatched, their young are blind and naked. The order contains three closely related families: hummingbirds, swifts, and tree swifts.

There are more than 300 hummingbird species, all of which live in the Americas and the Caribbean. Most prefer warm climates, but a few breed in Canada and Alaska. Hummingbirds have long, thin beaks and long tongues, which they dip into tubular flowers to feed on nectar, lapping it up with their tongues. They also eat small insects. All hummingbirds are tiny. The world's largest hummingbird is the giant hummingbird of South America. It weighs up to

Hummingbird feet are bare and lack the scalelike scutes found on other birds.

Swifts are built to spend long periods of time in the air.

0.9 ounces (25 g).[1] The smallest is the bee hummingbird of Cuba, which weighs only as much as 0.09 ounces (2.6 g).[2]

Swifts are larger than hummingbirds, weighing 1.3 to 1.8 ounces (36–50 g).[3] Their feet are so tiny they cannot even perch. They spend most of their time in the air, where they catch insects. Swifts have forked tails and look like flying boomerangs. They nest on cliffs or in caves on all continents except Antarctica.

Tree swifts also spend much of their time in the air, catching insects. But they can perch, and they nest in trees. They have crested heads, and—like swifts—long pointed wings and forked tails. They live in Asia and Australia.

HUMMINGBIRD EVOLUTION

In 2014, Jim McGuire and Robert Dudley of the University of California, Berkeley, along with other authors, published a new family tree for the hummingbird order. They analyzed DNA from 284 species and organized the samples by similarity.[4] The greater the similarity between two birds' DNA sequences, the more closely related they are. They placed the species on a cladogram showing their relationships. A clade is a group of organisms that all evolved from a common ancestor. This is usually determined by DNA comparisons. Scientists show these relationships in an evolutionary tree called a cladogram. They concluded that modern-day hummingbirds split from swifts and tree swifts approximately 42 MYA. Though hummingbirds are now only found in the New World, fossil records dating from 28 to 34 MYA indicate relatives of the hummingbird once lived in Europe and Asia. They probably moved from Asia to North America by a land bridge across the Bering Strait between present-day Russia and Alaska.

The long-tailed sylph hummingbird has a short beak, so it may poke through a flower's base to reach nectar.

The hummingbird's ancestors then followed the land route from North to South America, where they arrived approximately 22 MYA.

Hummingbird diversity exploded quickly in South America as adaptive radiation occurred. In this process, animals rapidly spread into new niches and form new species. Nine separate groups of hummingbirds developed new species to fill local ecological niches. South America's Andes Mountains became a center for hummingbird evolution. Although all hummingbirds feed on nectar, variations in beak shapes and coevolution in flower shapes drove the evolution of species diversity. Today, up to 25 species can live in the same area, each adapted to feed on nectar from different plants. According to McGuire, it is surprising that hummingbirds are so specific about where their nectar comes from. He says, "One of the really cool features of hummingbird evolution is that they all eat the same thing yet have diversified dramatically."[5]

This remarkably rapid hummingbird evolution is still occurring, albeit at a slightly slower pace. There are now 338 hummingbird species, but McGuire and Dudley think this number could double in the next several million years—a very short time in evolutionary history. According to Juan Francisco Ornelas of the Institute of Ecology in Xalapa, Mexico, "This is unique evidence of one of the most spectacular

HUMMINGBIRDS ARE EXTREME

"Everything about hummingbirds is extreme," says McGuire.[6] Their metabolic rate is the highest of any vertebrate. Their hippocampus is proportionally the largest of any bird. This brain structure controls spatial learning and helps birds return again and again to the same flower to feed. Hummingbirds hover in flight, beating their wings up to 80 times per second.[7] They migrate thousands of miles per year despite their tiny size. Even the variety in their iridescent color patterns is extreme.

RUBY-THROAT MIGRATION

Ruby-throated hummingbirds spend the winter in southern Mexico or northern Panama. They begin moving north in January. Males leave approximately ten days before females. By February, they reach Yucatán, Mexico, where they gorge on insects before flying to the United States. Some travel along the Texas coast, but most cross the Gulf of Mexico, which is a nonstop trip of up to 500 miles (800 km). Depending on weather, the trip takes 18 to 22 hours.[10] Birds may fly alone or in the occasional company of other birds. Sometimes they rest on oil rigs or fishing boats. By the time they reach land somewhere between southern Texas and Florida, they have lost half their body weight.

Ruby-throats are solitary. They neither live nor migrate in flocks, and they migrate over a period of approximately three months. This staggered migration prevents a major weather event from wiping out the entire species. Ruby-throats travel approximately 20 miles (32 km) per day before finally arriving at their home location somewhere in the eastern United States or southern Canada.[11]

known examples of an incomplete adaptive radiation."[8]

HUMMINGBIRDS AND MIGRATION

Migration is the seasonal movement of birds or other animals from one location to another to escape winter weather and find food. Tiny hummingbirds are intrepid migrators. Ruby-throated hummingbirds spend the spring and summer in the eastern United States and migrate 1,200 miles (1,900 km)—sometimes nonstop—to Central America for the winter.[9]

Hummingbirds began as tropical birds in Central and South America. As the glaciers receded, they expanded northward into the United States and Canada. During the winter they return to the tropics, where food is abundant. Hummingbird migration is not well documented, but studies indicate that the tiny birds have excellent navigation skills. Research suggests that individual birds fly alone and follow the same route every year, arriving at the same location on the same day as in previous years. First-year hummingbirds make the trip alone, without parental guidance.

Hummingbird migration appears to be triggered by the length of daylight. As the days get shorter in late summer, hummingbirds prepare for migration by feeding voraciously and increasing their body weight by 25 to 40 percent. Even with stored fat, most hummingbirds use so much energy that they stop often along the way to feed. That's because their hearts beat as many as 1,260 times per minute while they're flying and because their wings flap 15 to 80 times per second. Hummingbirds can travel up to 23 miles (37 km) per day when pushed by tailwinds.[12] These winds from behind speed their flight and decrease energy use. Even so, they fly close to the ground to better locate food sources during their travels.

HUMMINGBIRDS AND POLLINATION

With the highest metabolic rate of any bird, hummingbirds need a constant supply of energy. Besides flower nectar and tiny insects, some hummingbird stomachs also contain 10 to

15 percent pollen, although it is not known whether they feed on pollen deliberately or accidentally.[13] In any case, the hummingbird-pollen connection is vital for one of the hummingbird's primary tasks: pollination, or moving pollen between flowers to enable the plants to reproduce.

As hummingbirds stick their long beaks into tubular flowers for nectar, pollen grains attach to the sides of the beak. Depending on the flower, the birds' heads may also get dusted with pollen. When they visit the next flower, pollen grains rub off and pollinate the new plant. Because they visit 1,000 to 2,000 flowers every day, hummingbirds are highly efficient pollinators.[14]

Hummingbirds and their nectar sources have evolved together over the millennia in

A TASTE FOR SWEETNESS

The hummingbird's reliance on sugary nectar has earned it the reputation of having the bird equivalent of a sweet tooth. For an animal's sensory system to perceive a flavor, it must have a receptor to detect that flavor. The typical vertebrate receptor for sweet taste is a protein called TIR2. Hummingbirds lack this receptor. Instead, they have adapted another receptor, TIR1-TIR3, which normally detects savory taste, to detect sweetness. In the time since hummingbirds diverged from insect-eating swifts, this receptor has been repurposed to detect sugars.

a process called coevolution. One example of this is the carib hummingbird and the *Heliconia* plant. The tropical *Heliconia*, nicknamed lobster claws or parrot flowers, have large, brightly colored leaf structures surrounding their tiny flowers. To reach the nectar inside, carib hummingbirds have evolved beaks of various lengths and shapes—straight or curved—to best fit their chosen *Heliconia* flower. Adaptations of both birds and flowers vary on different Caribbean islands. Beak sizes also vary based on when the bird was alive. Those from the 1920s might be larger or smaller than those from the 1970s. Beak sizes also match flower changes.

Scientists don't know whether beak or flower changes came first, but over time, the two have adapted to each other. "It is probably best to view the interaction between these hummingbirds and their flowers as a dynamic one, in which each party can drive the evolution of the other," says Ethan J. Temeles of Amherst College.[15]

Hummingbirds are among the most distinctive and diverse birds in the world. They are also among the most watched and appreciated. The multitude of hummingbird feeders dotting the human landscape every summer may influence current and future hummingbird evolution by providing habitat and food sources for hummingbirds as natural food sources disappear with human development or climate change.

The waved albatross typically lives by the Galápagos Islands in South America. It is the only albatross that lives in the tropics.

CHAPTER FIVE

Tubenoses and Penguins

The order Procellariiformes, or tubenoses, includes approximately 100 species of petrels, albatrosses, and shearwaters.[1] These birds live at sea and visit land only to breed on remote islands or coastal cliffs. This makes them some of the most mysterious members of the bird kingdom. The 24 species of albatrosses are found in all oceans except the North Atlantic.[2] All but three breed in the Southern Hemisphere. Shearwaters, too, range across all oceans. The sooty shearwater, for example, migrates nearly 40,000 miles (64,000 km per year) from New Zealand to the North Pacific Ocean.[3] Many petrel species are also migratory, with a variety of species found across all oceans.

FLIGHT AND EGG SHAPE

A bird's egg surrounds a developing embryo with membranes, fluid, and a shell. Bird eggs range from almost perfectly round to teardrop shaped. New research suggests egg shape is linked with flying ability. Strong fliers lay streamlined eggs, which are more like ovals. This shape enables the egg to hold a larger chick without increasing its width, which would increase wind resistance as the bird flies. Because egg shape is based on flight ability, very different birds—hummingbirds and albatrosses, for example—have eggs of similar oval shapes. The red jungle fowl, the wild ancestor of domestic chickens, is not a strong flier. Its eggs are shaped more like spheres.

Tubenoses glide and soar on the sea winds and snatch food from the ocean surface. Their nickname describes a shared characteristic: nostrils enclosed in tubes that run the length of their beaks, opening at the beak tip. A gland at the base of their beaks removes excess salt from the water, and the tubular nostrils release this salt, which allows tubenoses to safely drink seawater.

TUBENOSE CHARACTERISTICS

Tubenoses are built for constant long-distance flying and gliding. They have long, slender, pointed wings and wide wingspans. The largest tubenose is the wandering albatross. It has a wingspan up to 12 feet (3.7 m). The smallest, the least storm petrel, has a wingspan of only one foot (0.3 m).[4] Tubenoses form strong, long-lasting relationships with a single mate. They lay one egg per mating. After the young leaves the nest, it stays at sea for five to ten years, depending on the species, until it is ready to breed.[5]

Albatrosses are huge, graceful birds. They can soar for hours without rest and without flapping their wings. Occasionally they float on the ocean surface, although this makes them vulnerable to predators. They eat schooling fish and squid and sometimes follow ships to pick up garbage.

Shearwaters and petrels are close relatives. They are more distantly related to albatrosses. They are similar to albatrosses in appearance, with long, stiff wings that enable them to glide for hours. They are so well adapted for flight that they are unable to properly walk on land. Petrels tend to be dark, small birds that fly low over the ocean. Shearwaters look much more like albatrosses—large, with long, slender wings. They are named for their stiff-winged gliding style that almost appears to “shear” the tops of the waves. Although closely related to petrels, their beaks are longer and more slender. Highly social birds, they form large, noisy feeding flocks at sea and gather in nesting colonies numbering in the millions.

EVOLUTION OF TUBENOSES

Scientists think ancient tubenoses first split off from another group of aquatic birds during the Cretaceous. The split that led to modern albatrosses and petrels occurred approximately 44.4 MYA. The earliest evidence of an albatross-like bird comes from a fossil found in South Carolina that dates to the Paleogene. Another, from the more recent Neogene period (23–2.6 MYA), was found in the United Kingdom. Most fossils are from the Atlantic and Pacific Oceans. Southern fossils are scarcer but have been found in Argentina, South Africa, and Australia, which suggests that the group was distributed worldwide. Shearwaters separated from other tubenoses beginning approximately 15 MYA and eventually separated into northern and southern groups.

There is controversy about tubenose evolution. Several studies have classified petrel groups differently in relation to each other and to albatrosses. Future studies may cause changes in classifications, but scientists now believe that modern-day albatrosses might have evolved from a small ancestor similar to a storm petrel. However, albatrosses and petrels are now separated into different clades based on different common ancestors.

Shearwaters are divided into several clades, but controversy about their exact relationships still exists. One group, the genus *Puffinus*, seems fairly well established. It can be divided into

Some penguins, including the African penguin, still live in warm climates like their ancestors did.

large-bodied and small-bodied clades that diverged approximately 10 MYA. The large-bodied clade includes the great and the sooty shearwaters. The small-bodied clade includes the Manx and the little, or dusky, shearwaters. Difficulties in locating and studying shearwaters have resulted in scarce and often conflicting data.

PENGUINS

It seems unlikely, but one of the bird clades most closely related to the tubenoses are the flightless penguins. According to a large 2014 DNA study that developed a new classification of bird groups, penguins are more closely related to albatrosses, petrels, and shearwaters than to any other birds.

The oldest known penguin-like fossil is approximately 60 to 62 million years old. This ancient penguin, *Waimanu manneringi*, could not fly and had short wings suitable for diving. But it did not much resemble modern penguins. By approximately 55 MYA, penguins were adapted to life in the water, but in a warmer environment than the polar regions where most modern penguins live. The basal penguin—the earliest common penguin ancestor that existed before modern penguins but after the evolution of flying birds—probably originated in the region of Gondwana that is now New Zealand.

PENGUIN RADIATION

A descendant of the basal penguin called Penguin One lived between 34.2 and 47.6 MYA. It is the ancestor of all of today's penguins. Penguin One successively gave rise to at least three more ancestors, Penguins A, B, and C. Approximately 40 MYA, Penguin A appeared, diverging into today's emperor and king penguins. Penguin B arose later and led to gentoo, Adélie, and chinstrap penguins. Penguin C gave rise to the Galápagos, Humboldt, Magellanic, and African penguins. Another unknown ancestor gave rise to the rest.

Over the next three million years, penguins began to diversify from this group of ancestors and filled ecological niches of recently extinct marine reptiles. Most food was in the oceans, which provided a strong selective advantage for birds to adapt to a swimming life. Wings shortened and became shaped like flaps; feathers became denser. These ancient penguins were, like today's penguins, warm-blooded birds that ate fish and krill.

Penguins live in polar regions because there are few land predators there. Recent DNA studies show many gene changes that adapt penguins to extreme cold. Genes code for proteins that cause dense packing of the penguin's short, stiff feathers. Both the feathers and their density improve insulation and waterproofing. Another gene thickens the skin. Genes that cause efficient fat storage enable penguins to withstand cold and go months without food.

The very different evolutionary paths of tubenoses and penguins, which started from the same ancestors, reflect different adaptations to ocean food sources. Catching food requires energy, and evolution favors adaptations that make food gathering more efficient. Tubenoses took to the air and became expert fliers. They viewed the ocean from above and scooped up prey from its surface. Penguins became expert swimmers and divers, seeking their prey nearer shore but deeper in the water. Emperor penguins, for example, can hold their breath for 20 minutes and dive up to 1,500 feet (460 m).[6] Though they are outwardly different, both kinds of birds are highly successful in their ocean habitats.

Stilts have long legs that allow them to wade in deep water.

CHAPTER SIX

Shorebirds and Waterfowl

As their name would suggest, many shorebirds live on the shores of oceans and lakes. Another large group, waterfowl, lives by rivers, lakes, and other freshwater bodies. Both groups migrate, stopping at ponds, wetlands, and other small water bodies along the way.

SEPARATING SHOREBIRDS AND WATERFOWL

Shorebirds, which are in the order Charadriiformes, are highly diverse. There are at least 57 species regularly seen in the United States.[1] Four common groups are oystercatchers, stilts and avocets, plovers, and sandpipers. Terns and gulls are also shorebirds.

EVOLUTION OF MIGRATION

Hundreds of bird species migrate every fall, traveling from warm, temperate breeding grounds to the tropics, where food and sunlight are plentiful, and returning the following spring. Some tiny birds cross entire oceans and continents.

The ancestors of migrating birds remained in the same place all year. Some scientists think tropical birds gradually moved north to flee competitors or exploit food sources. Others think temperate birds moved south to escape harsh winters. Lack of fossils makes it difficult to decide which hypothesis is correct.

University of Chicago scientists have built a mathematical model based on the ranges of modern birds and their evolutionary relationships. They hope to use the model to reconstruct the ranges of the birds' ancestors. For example, tests on migrating songbirds suggest that migrants were twice as likely to have originated in the temperate zone and moved south to the tropics. Some northern species eventually became full-time tropical residents.

Most shorebirds have relatively long legs and beaks. They feed in salt marshes and other coastal environments, eating fish and invertebrates.

Waterfowl, order Anseriformes, include ducks, geese, and swans. Waterfowl have short legs, webbed feet, waterproof feathers, and large, broad beaks. Most are vegetarians, feeding on grass or waterweeds, but swans and some ducks also feed on fish and insects. Waterfowl are strong swimmers and strong fliers, migrating hundreds or thousands of miles every year. Many ducks spend summers in northern Canada and Alaska and winters in the southern United States and Mexico. Other small groups of waterfowl include grebes, mergansers, and teals.

The *V. iaai* fossil included the creature's vocal organ. Because of its similarities to duck vocal organs, researchers believe it would have sounded like a duck.

WATERFOWL AND SHOREBIRD EVOLUTION

More than 65 MYA, dinosaurs kept company with a bird named *Vegavis iaai*, which then lived on after dinosaurs died out. *Vegavis iaai* is a member of the order Anseriformes and a relative of waterfowl, but it is not a direct ancestor of modern ducks and geese. Still, its fossils, found in Antarctica in 1992, prove that relatives of today's ducks coexisted with nonavian dinosaurs. Before this find, scientists did not know whether ancestors of modern birds lived at that time.

Wood ducks eat insects, seeds, and fruits.

A major factor driving the evolution of birds was diet, which led to variations in beak size and shape. Aaron Olsen of Brown University is fascinated by the proliferation of beak types in ducks and geese. Olsen made 3-D measurements of 136 skulls and beaks in 51 species of living and extinct waterfowl.[2] One of these was *Presbyornis*, which lived in the Paleogene.

When Olsen cross-referenced these measurements with the birds' diets and feeding habits, he found that diet and beak shape are linked. Duck beaks are relatively long, with wide tips that allow ducks to take in water and filter out food. The shorter, narrower beaks of geese are useful for browsing on plant roots and leaves. The *Presbyornis* beak shape is similar to the duck beak, leading Olsen to believe that early Anseriformes ancestors were duck-like and that goose beaks evolved later.

GIANT PREHISTORIC GOOSE

The region including London, Essex, and Kent in the United Kingdom was once ocean. Flying over those waters 50 MYA was *Dasornis*, a goose the size of a small plane. Its wingspan was more than 16 feet (5 m), and it had bony pseudoteeth made of fingernail-like keratin rather than enamel and dentin.[3] These teeth probably helped it hold on to fish and squid that could wriggle loose from a beak. Though *Dasornis*'s lifestyle was apparently much like that of today's albatrosses, it was most closely related to ducks and geese.

GOOSE HYBRIDIZATION

If two organisms are members of different species, they should not be able to interbreed successfully. But hybrids—individuals resulting from mating between two species—are fairly common, especially among birds such as geese, in which males have retained a penis, which many birds do not have. In the United Kingdom, hybridization (pictured) commonly occurs between native graylag geese and Canada geese, an invading North American species. Two behaviors in these species favor hybridization. While females typically choose mates, males sometimes override their choices by forcing themselves on females, regardless of species. Second, some females have more eggs than they can care for. These females may lay the excess eggs in other species' nests. That species cares for the young, which are more likely to mate with the species that raises them.

In general, birds have large eyes and excellent vision, including better color vision than mammals. Shorebirds have especially excellent color vision. Humans have three types of cone cells in the eye to distinguish three colors: red, green, and blue. Birds have more cone cells than humans, plus a fourth type to distinguish ultraviolet, or UV, light, which humans cannot see.

Studies of the visual proteins of gulls and terns show that they have a visual pigment in the eye that is both violet sensitive (VS) and ultraviolet sensitive (UVS). The VS pigment absorbs light at slightly longer wavelengths and appears to be the version present in bird ancestors. It is more common in birds than the UVS version, which has developed

Excellent vision is important to help birds avoid hitting things while flying and to help them catch prey.

independently several times in shorebirds and several other bird orders. UV vision likely aids birds in locating and recognizing prey and mates. In one case, evolutionary biologist Tim Birkhead watched a murre—a seabird—recognize her mate when to Birkhead's vision the mate appeared as a tiny blob hundreds of yards out at sea. Specialized vision is just one of the adaptations birds have that help them survive.

The bald eagle is one of many species of raptor.

CHAPTER SEVEN

Birds of Prey

Birds of prey, also called raptors, survive by eating other animals. They have extremely keen eyesight thanks to large eyes and full color vision. Their legs are strong and end in sharp talons that can grasp, carry, and even crush prey. Their sharp, curved beaks are designed to tear flesh. It might seem as though all birds having these uniquely terrifying characteristics would be closely related. But they are not.

BIRD OF PREY ORDERS

Two orders of raptors are diurnal, or active during the day. The order Accipitriformes includes hawks, eagles, osprey, kites, and vultures. The order Falconiformes includes falcons, falconets, kestrels, and caracaras. Sometimes *raptors* is used only to refer to these two groups. Although these orders look and behave much alike, a 2015

CONVERGENT EVOLUTION

Convergent evolution of flight occurred in many animals, including pterosaurs, birds, and bats. Pterosaurs, or flying reptiles, probably originated from a bipedal, running ancestor. They likely developed flight from the ground up; that is, they began as runners. They developed a keeled breastbone, an elongated fourth digit, and wing fibers analogous to feathers. Birds came from predatory dinosaurs that were also bipedal runners. They developed adaptations similar to pterosaurs—a keeled breastbone, hollow bones, and feathers rather than fibers. Rather than an elongated fourth digit, elongations of the arm and wrist bones support bird feathers. The bats' common ancestor is unknown but may have been a tree-dwelling glider. Bats evolved extremely efficient flight by elongating all digits in the hand and developing thin membranes between them.

DNA study involving 198 bird species suggests they are not very closely related.[1] Falcons are much closer to parrots and perching birds than to hawks and eagles. A third group of raptors are owls in the order Strigiformes. They are nocturnal, or active at night. Their large eyes, which face forward and have high concentrations of rod cells, give them excellent night vision. Despite their special nocturnal adaptations, owls are genetically much more closely related to hawks and eagles than they are to falcons.

Falcons branched off from a completely different group of bird ancestors than did the other two raptor orders. That is, while the hawk and owl orders appear close together on the phylogenetic tree, falcons appear in a separate location. Scientists suggest two ways falcons could have been separated. First, all three groups could have developed carnivorous, raptor-like characteristics independently through convergent evolution. This is a process by which unrelated or distantly related groups of organisms evolve similar characteristics. The second theory is that a very distant ancestor of all three groups was a predator. Raptors simply kept the ancestral characteristics, while groups related to falcons, such as parrots, lost them. Scientists currently favor the second hypothesis.

TERROR BIRDS

The original dinosaur ancestors of birds, the theropods, were predators. But only some birds are predators. One of the most intimidating ancient bird predators, known as the terror bird, had a head much like today's hawks and eagles but was huge and flightless. The terror bird reigned as South America's top predator from 60 MYA—shortly after large dinosaurs disappeared—until just 2.5 MYA.

The 17 species of terror birds were South America's only large predators.[2] They charged through the landscape, gorging themselves on the continent's many herbivorous mammals. Terror birds included the world's biggest bird species, the largest of which was unearthed in Argentina in 2006. When living, this 15-million-year-old bird stood ten feet (3 m) tall. Its head

An artist depicts a terror bird taking down a prehistoric horse, which was smaller than today's horse.

was the size of a horse's head, with a 2.5-foot (0.8 m) skull. Its giant nose and sharp, curving, eagle-like beak measured 18 inches (46 cm) long.[3] These huge, hooked beaks could snap the spinal cord of a horse with a single bite. Other terror birds were much smaller, ranging from two to three feet (0.6 to 0.9 m) tall.[4]

Terror birds had rock-hard skulls. In addition to snapping necks, some might have stunned or killed their prey by head-butting it. Others may have killed by kicking or stomping prey with their *T. rex*-like feet. Although no one is sure exactly how terror birds killed their prey, they had plenty of weapons, and killing methods likely varied by body size.

Luis Chiappe, director of the Dinosaur Institute at the Natural History Museum of Los Angeles County, California, was one discoverer of the Argentinian terror bird. Chiappe thinks the birds were good runners despite their large size. He estimates their speed as similar to present-day emus but slower than ostriches, today's fastest birds. Emus run up to 30 miles per hour (48 kmh). Ostriches reach 43 miles per hour (69 kmh).[5]

EVOLUTION OF RAPTOR BEAKS AND PLUMAGE

There are many examples among birds of beak shapes adapted to diet. The Galápagos finches first studied by Darwin include 13 species that evolved from a single type of ancestor.[6] They

FAST-TRACKING EVOLUTION?

Snail kites live in central Florida, where they have traditionally fed on apple snails. The kites use their long, hooked beaks to pull snails from their shells. But in 2005, a larger snail invaded from South America and began to replace apple snails. In less than a decade, or approximately 1.5 snail kite generations, the kite population had larger beaks, making them able to eat the larger snails.[7] Is this evolution? Not yet, according to University of Florida scientists studying the phenomenon. Parents don't seem to be necessarily passing along long beaks to their offspring. But they soon could be. Even in the first year, larger kites and larger-beaked kites showed better survival rates than smaller ones. If larger snails continue to dominate, natural selection will soon lead to an increased proportion of large beaks in the kite population—that is, evolution will occur.

lived on the Galápagos Islands off the coast of Ecuador. Individuals were isolated on different islands and used food sources available to them, including seeds, nectar, insects, and blood from iguanas. Over time, the size and shape of the birds' beaks changed to fit each food source. But this type of response to diet does not occur in birds of prey. Beak changes in raptors are tied to factors other than diet, including the shape of the skull.

According to a 2016 study, skull and beak shape in raptors are tightly linked by genetics. A change in one can occur only with a change in the other. Songbirds, such as finches, seem able to break this connection, but raptors do not, says Dr. Jen Bright, lead author of the study. Coauthor Jesus Marugán-Lobón adds, "Basically, if you're a bird of prey and you're small, you look like a tiny falcon, and if you're a bird of prey and you're large, your skull looks like a vulture."[8]

The study concludes that this relationship between evolution of raptor beaks and skull shape accounts for approximately 80 percent of the beak and skull changes observed in raptors.[9] In general, if feeding habits change, the size of the entire bird changes. Birds with long, narrow beaks and flat skulls—vultures and eagles, for example—tend to be larger. Smaller falcons have shorter beaks and wider, more rounded skulls.

Although skulls and beaks are very constant within a species, members of some raptor species show color polymorphism, or variations in feather color. These color variations are not tied to gender or age. One member of a species might be brown while another is gray. Falcons and owls often show color polymorphism. Many scientists thought polymorphism was related to diet. They suspected prey animals were less likely to recognize predators with a different plumage mutation. This would give polymorphic predators a selective advantage, so some would remain in the population.

But a study looking to tie polymorphism in hawks and owls with different factors, including diet, showed that diet had little effect. Instead, polymorphism was strongly connected with

Eastern screech owls can be gray or red.

population size. Mutations, or genetic changes, are more likely to appear in larger populations. Polymorphism also decreased with breeding altitude. That is, the higher in altitude, or farther from sea level, the species lived and bred, the less likely it was to show color polymorphism. Additionally, bird species living closer to the poles showed more polymorphism than those nearer the equator. Both results are also correlated to population size, since a bird's range and population size tend to be larger at low altitudes and larger near the poles than near the equator. These changes all help birds of prey fit their environments.

TAWNY OWLS RESPOND TO CLIMATE CHANGE

Birds continue to evolve in response to today's environmental changes. One example is the European tawny owl, which has been visibly affected by climate change. This owl is polymorphic, with two color patterns, light gray and reddish brown. Tawny owls in cold, snowy Finland are mostly gray. But for the past 50 years, as snowfall has decreased, the number of reddish-brown birds is increasing.[10] As Europe warms, scientists expect this trend to continue. There will be less advantage for the gray coloration, which camouflages owls in snow.

Many parrots, including lorikeets, are known for their brilliant colors.

CHAPTER EIGHT

Parrots and Kin

The order Psittaciformes includes more than 350 species of birds, including parrots, macaws, Amazons, lorikeets, lovebirds, cockatoos, and parakeets.[1] All parrots have short, broad, curved beaks, which they use to eat fruit, flowers, nuts, seeds, and insects. Most parrots live in warm, tropical regions around the world, especially Australasia—comprising Australia, New Zealand, and surrounding Pacific islands—and Central and South America. Parrots have zygodactyl feet, with the first and fourth toes pointing backward and the second and third toes pointing forward. Woodpeckers and owls also have zygodactyl feet, which are good for clinging to tree trunks and perching on branches. Parrot life spans vary, but some live up to 80 years in the wild.[2]

People value parrots as pets because of their beauty and bright colors, high intelligence, and mimicry abilities. Many can develop large vocabularies and speak in sentences. Parrots are affectionate and form strong bonds with their human keepers. Betty Jean Craige owns a female African gray parrot named Cosmo, who mimics the birds and squirrels in the woods outside. She also talks. Cosmo will enter Craige's study, climb onto her cage, and announce, "Here I am." When she wants affection, she says, "Betty Jean kiss feathers, OK?" or "We're gonna go to cuddle?" Craige says, "Her grammar was not perfect, but her message was clear."[3]

KEA PARROTS

The kea lives in snowy mountain passes in New Zealand rather than in the tropics. Keas are omnivores and eat a variety of plant matter, insect larvae, carrion, and birds. Occasionally, they even prey on sheep. They land on a sheep's back and peck through skin and muscle to reach the fat around the kidneys, which sometimes kills the sheep. A bounty on keas led to 150,000 keas being shot between 1860 and 1970.[4] This killing put them on the New Zealand endangered species list. But these highly intelligent birds are now protected.

Cosmo is not unique. African grays are known for their intelligence and ability to talk. The most famous is probably Alex, who lived and talked with his owner, Irene Pepperberg, for 30 years before his unexpected death in 2007. Alex even made television appearances. But most of all, he showed that parrots are more than just mimics—they think, reason, and understand concepts. When asked what color corn is without corn in the room, Alex would say, "Yellow."[5] He understood color, corn, and yellow even without examples in front of him.

EARLY PARROTS

Parrots are an ancient group, but their uniqueness has made it difficult to accurately determine their nearest relatives. Recent studies show they are most closely related to perching birds, both of which branched off from falcons. The oldest known parrot fossil dates back about 50 million years, but new DNA evidence suggests parrots originated in the Cretaceous, about 80 MYA.

Studying the order Psittaciformes is somewhat easier than studying other bird orders because parrots do not migrate. This makes it easier to uncover their patterns of diversification. An extensive study by a team from the University of New Mexico and the Smithsonian analyzed DNA from 69 parrot genera and several bird orders thought to be related.[6] The scientists concluded that parrots originated in Australasia during the Cretaceous when this region was still part of the Gondwana supercontinent. The orders of pigeons and perching birds likely originated during this time as well.

The oldest known split in the parrot order occurred in New Zealand. Three species, now considered their own family, split off. These are the kea (*Nestor notabilis*), the kaka (*Nestor meridionalis*), and the kakapo (*Strigops habroptilis*). The kea is unusual because it lives in the mountains. The closely related kaka lives in lowland forests. Both are large and very intelligent. The flightless kakapo is the world's heaviest parrot, weighing more than 6.6 pounds (3 kg).[7] It is now critically endangered, or close to extinction.

Cockatoos also split off early from other parrot groups, yet exactly when is still uncertain. Comparisons of DNA from 69 living parrot species, plus eight additional bird orders, suggest it happened somewhere between 65 and 45 MYA. Other groups then separated until all major lineages were present by 30 MYA, when Australia, Antarctica, and South America had completely separated from Gondwana. Adaptive radiation of South American parrots probably began by approximately 33 MYA. Fossils of modern-day parrots have been found from the Neogene, and a fossil from 20 MYA found in Wyoming was a member of genus *Conuropsis*, the same as the recently extinct Carolina parakeet. A cockatoo from Australia dated back to 15 MYA, and parakeets from Australia and Argentina dated to less than 5 MYA.

The kakapo forages for food including fruit, flowers, seeds, and leaves.

PARROT COLORS AND MIMICRY

What makes parrot colors so outstanding? First, parrots are one of only a few bird groups that have powder down. This specialized type of down feather breaks down to form a powder used in preening. Second, the blue colors are structural. Structural colors occur when layers of melanin granules and the protein keratin are stacked in the feathers, giving off a bright-blue appearance when light reflects off them. Carotenoid pigments, the same pigment that colors carrots, cause the red or yellow coloration found in most birds. Parrots also have unique pigments called psittacofulvins. Scientists have not yet determined the chemical structure of this class of pigments.

Many factors drive the evolution of color in birds. One factor is sexual selection. Males develop bright, noticeable color patterns to impress females and improve mating success. But the brighter the bird, the more visible it is to both predators and prey. This problem can be handled evolutionarily in several ways. In the tropics, where most parrots live, bright coloration can act as camouflage. In the bright rain forest canopy, yellows and greens blend in better than duller colors. Birds that live closer to the rain forest floor have more muted colors, such as browns. Scientists at Chicago's Peggy Notebaert Nature Museum also point out that the tropics have more birds of all kinds. Rain forests are incredibly diverse and have many colorful birds, but

Many parrots have brightly colored feathers.

even more dull-brown ones. The many rain forest niches enable both brilliant parrots and little brown birds to blend in.

The ability to mimic calls also serves a purpose. Michael Schindlinger of Lesley University points out that many birds know their species' calls instinctively. But mimics learn calls from

Many parrots, including eclectus parrots, can mimic human words.

listening to those around them. Captive parrots listen to humans. Wild parrots pick up the calls of their parents and other members of their species. Parrots develop local dialects, or variations in the usual calls, which may help males and females find each other or help territorial competitors avoid each other. They react most strongly to their local dialect. Parrots and other mimics must have good hearing and memories, plus good muscle control to produce specific sounds.

Biologist Karl Berg has proven that each individual parrot has its own name. Using cameras and sound recordings in their nests, he showed that hatchlings of the green-rumped parrotlet each learn and recognize their parents' names and develop their own names. By switching eggs from one nest to another, he also showed that hatchlings develop names similar to those of their adoptive parents rather than the names of their biological parents—in other words, the names are learned, not instinctive.

Parrots' ability to mimic sounds around them is evidence of their intelligence and ability to learn. Comparative studies are needed to understand how and why mimicry happens evolutionarily. However, especially in the case of parrots, the opportunity to do such studies is at risk as parrots are brought closer to extinction by habitat loss and poaching for the pet trade.

THE PET TRADE AND EXTINCTION

A major cause of wildlife extinction is capture for the pet trade. Parrots are particularly valued. At least 259 parrot species have been traded around the world, and almost 30 percent of the 355 species are now threatened with extinction.[8] Bans on legal trading have led to a booming parrot-poaching trade in some countries, including Mexico. Poachers take parrots illegally. Parrots are targeted because people enjoy their sizes, colors, and ability to speak. Amazon parrots and macaws bring in the most money and are caught most often. They are the most threatened. At least one species, the Spix's macaw, went extinct in the wild when poachers took too many.

Waxwings belong to the order Passeriformes.

CHAPTER NINE

Perching Birds

By far the largest, most diverse bird order is the order Passeriformes. These birds are known as passerines, or perching birds. This huge group includes a large subsection known as songbirds. Today, of the more than 10,000 total bird species, nearly 6,000 are perching birds.[1] They live everywhere in the world except Antarctica and are most diverse in the tropics. They are generally small. The largest—ravens—reach weights of approximately three pounds (1.4 kg).[2]

Despite their diversity, all passerines form a single clade, which means they all descended from a common ancestor. All have a set of distinguishing traits, including unique structures of sperm cells, bony palates, and muscles of the wings and legs. The most obvious feature is the one they are named for. All perching birds have four toes oriented so the first toe, or hallux, points backward and the other

TWINS ON SEPARATE CONTINENTS

Sometimes convergent evolution produces amazing similarities on separate continents. The western meadowlark lives and nests on the ground in North American grasslands. It evolved from tree-dwelling blackbirds. The yellow-throated longclaw inhabits grasslands in West and South Africa. It evolved from Old World pipits, which are small brown songbirds that live and nest on the ground in open country. Today, neither western meadowlarks nor yellow-throated longclaws resemble their respective ancestors. Not only are they both ground dwellers, but their size, plumage colors, and markings also look almost exactly alike.

three point forward. These anisodactyl feet are extremely efficient for perching.

ANCESTORS, RELATIVES, AND PRESENT-DAY FAMILIES

Because passerines are so diverse, it is difficult to pinpoint the clades most closely related to passerines. Originally, they were thought to be closest to clades such as cuckoos, kingfishers, and woodpeckers, all of which have feet with two toes pointing forward and two backward. This presumed relationship was based on structural traits. Yet another classification based on DNA analysis suggested that sister groups of passerines included pigeons, doves, cranes, rails, and storks. But common ancestors with these groups occur far back in the evolutionary tree, indicating distant relationships. A 2008 study of DNA sequences places passerines closest in lineage to parrots and falcons. This set of relationships is currently accepted, but further study is needed.

Scientists think early passerines evolved approximately 55 to 60 MYA in Gondwana. Adaptive radiation began in Australasia and New Guinea, and the birds later expanded rapidly into Eurasia and Africa. Today, scientists recognize more than 100 different families of passerines. The number changes because scientific understanding of relationships constantly changes as new data emerges.

Passerines average the smallest in physical size of all bird orders (since swifts and hummingbirds are in the same order, swifts make the average size of that order larger than passerines). Scientists divide passerines into three suborders. The most ancient includes two species of New Zealand wrens, which branched off from all other passerines very early. A second group is the oscines and suboscines, commonly called songbirds. This is by far the largest group, comprising 5,000 of the approximately 6,000 species. Many familiar bird families are songbirds, including sparrows, finches, thrushes, swallows, starlings, warblers, larks, nightingales, lyrebirds, and crows and ravens. The final suborder is a catchall group containing the other 1,000 nonsongbirds.[3] They include several South American groups, such as tyrant flycatchers, cotingas, manakins, and ovenbirds. Old World nonsongbirds include broadbills and pittas.

Passerines are able to perch easily for long periods of time because of their special foot construction.

PERCHING TOES

The passerine toe configuration is unique in having an opposable toe—much like a thumb—that makes grasping easier. This helps passerines grasp not only branches but also food items such as seeds or insects. In their dinosaur ancestors, who moved by running instead of flying, this toe was small and unopposable. Because it did not touch the ground, fossil prints lack this toe.

The evolutionary development of the opposable toe is repeated in the development of bird embryos. Metatarsals, or foot bones, of chicken embryos grow most rapidly toward the proximal end, the end where they attach to the body. Early in development, the toe is straight, like dinosaur toes. But because the developing bones are still made of cartilage, they are highly plastic and thus able to move and twist. As the baby bird moves within the egg, the toe becomes twisted.

Thin tendons running from the leg muscles to the toes, which tighten when the bird lands and lock in place until it straightens its legs, also aid perching in passerines. The tendons keep the bird clinging to the branch even during sleep. Perching birds have small, unfeathered feet with few nerves or blood vessels. This means they have little feeling in their feet and can land on very cold perches, such as wires. They stay warm by sitting with their belly feathers covering their feet.

SONGBIRDS

Passerine songbirds are not the only birds that can sing; this ability has evolved separately, several times. Parrots and songbirds evolved birdsong and then diverged, but hummingbirds developed their ability to sing separately. A group of approximately 50 genes is involved in both birdsong and human speech.[4] Similar genes allow humans to speak and birds to sing. This is why some birds can so readily mimic human speech.

Birds vocalize using the syrinx, or voice box, which is a set of muscles surrounding the trachea. A bird's syrinx differs from the human larynx. The syrinx is located in the chest, just above the branching of the two bronchial tubes, rather than in the throat. It has two parts that connect separately to the two lungs. This enables the bird to produce sounds of two different frequencies simultaneously. Nonsongbirds have simple syrinx muscles. Their songs are not learned but are known instinctively and never vary. Similar to parrots, true songbirds learn their songs from birds around them. They remember and often improvise. Their vocalizations are possible because of the complexity of the syrinx muscles.

There are two types of bird vocalizations. One type, the call, is short and practical—used, for example, to signal danger. These songs are used all year. Songs that are longer and more complex are typically used only during breeding season. Some species have relatively simple songs and can learn new songs only during the first few months of life. Others learn new songs throughout their lives. Approximately one-third of songbird species sing only one song, but approximately 20 percent of all bird species have more than five. The brown thrasher, a relative of the mockingbird, sings more than 2,000 songs.[5] Like human speech, birdsong is learned in two stages. First, the young birds hear and memorize a tutor song or template. Then they practice, comparing their song to the template and refining it. Baby birds prevented from hearing their own species' songs develop abnormal songs.

Passerines have come a long way from their dinosaur ancestors, and they continue to evolve. They are among the most noticeable members of the animal community. Their bright colors, cheerful songs, and entertaining antics bring joy to bird-watchers everywhere.

CROWS AND RAVENS

Crows, ravens, and their relatives are very intelligent. Captive ravens were shown how to use a tool to obtain a treat from a box. Then, both box and tool were removed. Later, the ravens were given a choice of objects, including the tool. Still later, the box was returned. Eighty percent had chosen the right tool and retrieved a treat. When the experiment was repeated the next day, the success rate was 90 percent—more successful than four-year-old children.[6]

Wild crows also show intelligence and learning. Behaviorists Kaeli N. Swift and John M. Marzluff conducted a complex experiment to test how wild urban crows respond to predators. Crows were conditioned to find food in a given location. Then, in that location, they were presented with either a dead crow, a dead pigeon, a live red-tailed hawk (a predator), or both a dead crow and a hawk. When the crows saw either a dead crow, a hawk, or both, they mobbed together and took more time to approach food in these areas. When they saw a dead pigeon, they did not show these responses. They remembered places where crows had died and the predators in the area at the time.

Although rare, fossils of birds and even bird feathers provide valuable insight into bird evolution.

CHAPTER TEN

Present-Day Research

Bird evolution has had many recent breakthroughs. There is an explosion of research as scientists rush to fill in the blanks in a field once hampered by a lack of fossil evidence and good analytical techniques. Birds are often tiny, and their bones are hollow and thin. The chance that a bird skeleton will form a lasting fossil is small. The chance it will be found by a paleontologist millions of years later is even smaller. Compared to large dinosaurs or mammals, bird fossils are rare. Also, until recently, scientists had few tools to adequately study bird evolution. Not until development of technologies such as DNA analysis have scientists made significant steps in understanding the evolutionary relationships of birds.

NEW FOSSILS

Bird fossils are still comparatively rare, but scientists continue to find more. Since 2000, bird fossil discoveries have been made all over the world. Different discoveries from 2016 uncovered fossil bones of giant flightless birds in the Arctic, New Zealand, and Wyoming. An almost complete skeleton of a terror bird was found on an Argentinian beach in 2015. The fossil included the shape of the bird's beak, skull, and inner ear. These structures suggest that terror birds had deep voices and good hearing at low frequencies.

China has been a hotbed of fossil discovery. A duck-like diving bird that lived among dinosaurs 110 MYA was found in 2006. It has many characteristics of modern birds. The oldest known toothless bird was found in China in 2009. The pigeon-sized bird probably fed on fish and nested in trees. In 2004, a tiny, feathered enantiornithine bird from 121 MYA was found still in its egg.

A discovery in Burma, in Southeast Asia, gives an exquisite glimpse of bird life from 100 MYA. A just-hatched baby bird fell into a pool of amber tree sap. The amber beautifully preserved the enantiornithine hatchling, including most of its skull and neck, part of a wing and hind limb, soft tissues of the tail, and both flight feathers and tail feathers—enough to show many structural details. In Alaska's Denali National Park, a slab of rock contains many well-preserved fossil tracks of birds, pterosaurs, and dinosaurs dating back to 70 MYA. Each new discovery adds to scientists' understanding of how and where birds evolved.

NEW TECHNOLOGIES

Analyzing fossils is now possible using the same high-level technology used in medical research. This includes imaging techniques such as electron microscopy, which allows scientists to study fossils at the molecular level by magnifying them up to two million times. Another is computer-aided visualization such as synchrotron microtomography. In this process, paleontologists pass an energy source, such as

THE OLDEST BABY BIRD

Enantiornithines were an evolutionary dead end—none of their descendants survive today. But scientists know they had teeth, wings with clawed fingers, and feathers like modern bird feathers. And thanks to a very rare, two-inch (5 cm), 127-million-year-old baby bird fossil, scientists know they probably developed much like modern birds.[1] The fossil indicates the baby's breastbone was still cartilage, not bone, which meant it couldn't fly at the time of its death. It was probably highly dependent on its parents. Scientists learned these things by analyzing the baby bird's bones in a synchrotron, a technology not yet available when the fossil was found many years ago in Spain. Because the patterns of bone development in this baby differed from patterns in other baby enantiornithines, scientists think the group was probably more diverse than previously thought.

an X-ray, through the fossil to make a 3-D reconstruction of the specimen without damaging it. These 3-D reconstructions provide paleontologists with much more information about how the organism looked and functioned while alive. Scientists can use this information to test hypotheses on the functions and behaviors of long-extinct organisms. Newer technologies using higher-energy and higher-resolution scans can even produce 3-D images without removing the fossil from the rock in which it is found.

DNA analysis is likewise valuable in understanding evolution. In the 2000s, this has led to the new science of evolutionary genomics. Using genomics, or the analysis of large groups of genes, scientists can determine the relative times at which groups of species evolved and how closely species are related. In genomics, scientists analyze genomes, the

ANCIENT BIRDS SAW IN COLOR

Chinese scientists have shown that an ancient, now-extinct group of birds had excellent color vision. The sparrow-sized fossil they studied, a type of enantiornithine, had a beautifully preserved eye region. The living tissue was replaced with minerals, but when scientists viewed the eye with a scanning electron microscope, they observed droplets of oil. In modern birds, each cone, or color-sensing cell, has a droplet of oil at its tip that acts like a camera filter and improves color vision. Droplets in the fossil bird's eye were identical to those in modern birds. This suggests color vision was fully developed 120 MYA, when this bird lived.

Scientists use the ID19 microtomography beamline at the European Synchrotron Radiation Facility in France to create 3-D images of fossils.

complete sets of genes or entire DNA content for a given organism or species. They sequence the DNA, or determine the exact order of the nucleotide components in the genes. Then they compare DNA sequences of various species. If the DNA sequences match closely, the species are closely related and close in evolutionary time. Because the technologies of gene analysis have become so much better and faster, massive amounts of data can now be collected. Comparisons

ANCIENT BIRD COLORS

Paleontologists can now see colors in ancient bird fossils. Using a synchrotron, in 2011 a team of scientists from the University of Manchester, United Kingdom, scanned two well-preserved fossils: a 120-million-year-old *Confuciusornis sanctus*, the world's earliest beaked bird, and a 110-million-year-old *Gansus yumenensis*, the oldest modern bird fossil. Both fossils included copper bound into eumelanin, a dark pigment molecule. The pigment was perfectly preserved within the feather structure. This led scientists to the conclusion that *C. sanctus* had a black body and neck and patchy-colored wings.

Besides color patterns, the synchrotron also offers insight into ancient biochemistry, including clues about the birds' chemical reactions and the foods they ate. At Yale University, scientists used an electron microscope to examine feathers preserved in Germany 40 MYA. The feathers showed iridescent colors similar to those in today's starlings. The basic feather is black, but when turned at certain angles, it shows iridescent bluish, greenish, or coppery coloration. Using this new ability to see structures in very great detail, scientists hope to unlock more secrets of ancient bird and dinosaur coloration.

can be made involving the complete genomes of many species, and investigations can be done on the effects of selection on genomes.

AVIAN PHYLOGENOMICS CONSORTIUM

Scientists have known for years that birds survived the mass extinction of the dinosaurs approximately 65 MYA and that they evolved rapidly and radiated throughout the world. But since 2010, researchers have made significant progress in understanding how this occurred. In 2010, an international group of scientists, with leaders from China, Denmark, and the United States, formed the Avian Phylogenomics Consortium. The group includes more than 200 scientists from 80 institutions in 20 countries.

They use new technologies—particularly genomics—to help answer questions about how modern-day birds came to be. In one project, participating scientists sequenced, assembled, and compared the genomes of 48 species of birds, including representatives of all modern bird groups.[2]

In the past, scientists tried to tease out bird relationships using only ten to 20 genes.[3] But bird evolution was so rapid and genetic differences so small that this approach was not accurate. The whole genome approach has led to different conclusions and considerably more knowledge of bird origins. For example, the data suggests three separate origins for waterbirds, including waterfowl, shorebirds, and others, and indicates that the common ancestor of land birds was a top predator—and also the ancestor of South America's giant terror birds.

Genomic studies suggest that birds began their radiation approximately 66 MYA, just as large dinosaurs went extinct. They indicate that more than 10,000 bird species evolved in less than 15 million years, filling the many empty ecological niches opened by the extinction event.

Surprisingly, studies showed that birds have lost much of the DNA present in other reptiles. Bird genomes contain fewer repeating DNA sequences, and they lost hundreds of genes shortly after they split from other reptiles. For example, many of the lost genes are essential in the human respiratory system. According to Guojie Zhang, one of the study leaders, "The loss of these key genes may have a significant effect on the evolution of many distinct phenotypes of birds. This is an exciting finding, because it is quite different from what people normally think, which is that innovation is normally created by new genetic material, not the loss of it. Sometimes, less is more."[4]

The consortium released 29 papers in major science journals in 2014, but the group's work is just beginning as scientists tackle the many questions raised by new datasets.[5] Consortium scientists are collecting their results into a huge database that will be available for use by all scientists. This is the first attempt to use such large quantities of data in the study of a whole animal group. They hope it will serve as a model for future research.

Future research is likely to continue at a fast pace as scientists analyze and answer questions about past bird evolution. But it is also likely that some of ornithologists' energy will be directed to birds' present and future evolution. This is because human factors, including climate change, habitat loss, and pollution, are currently threatening bird populations and survival.

One way to measure human impacts on evolution is to look at extinction rates, which have risen significantly in the past 500 years. Scientists know of six bird species that went extinct

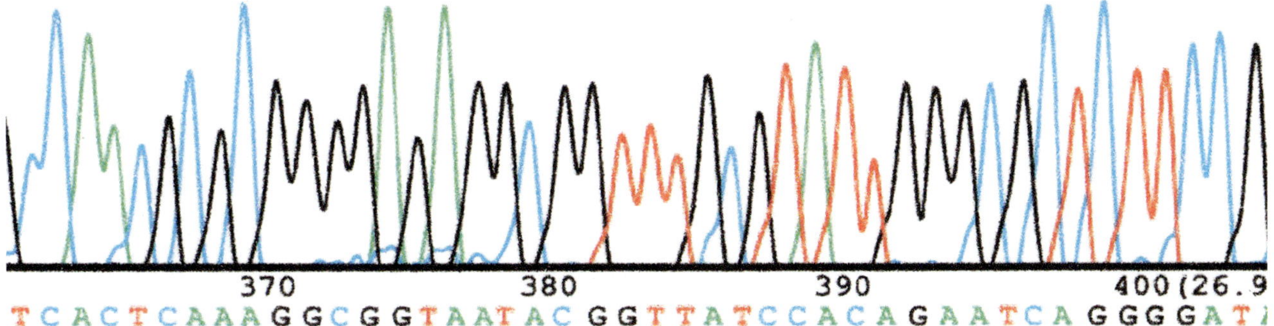

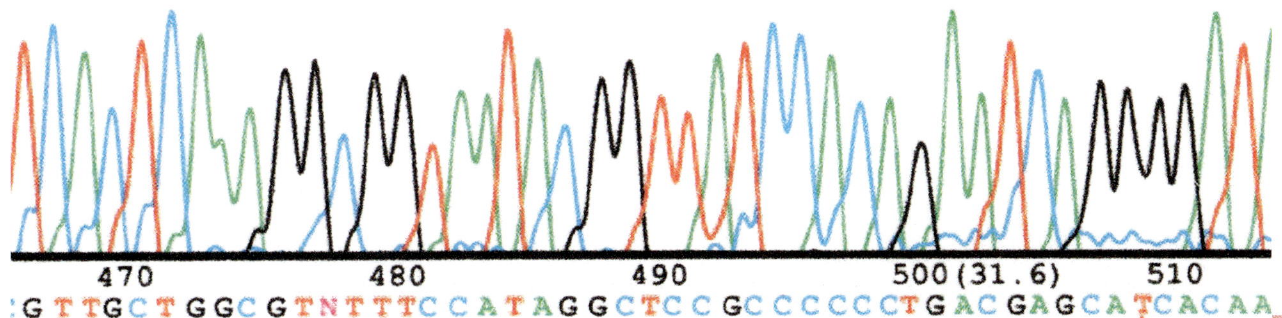

Scientists can chart out DNA sequences and use computers to help find repeated sequences.

before 1600. Ten more went extinct in the 1600s, 27 in the 1700s, 48 in the 1800s, and 63 in the 1900s.[6] These rates are far higher than naturally occurring rates. Unless humans change their ways, humans will cause Earth's sixth mass extinction. This will result in a great decline in bird species diversity. Stopping or slowing this decline would require efforts including increased conservation and slowing climate change. In short, the present and future evolution of birds rests less on natural selection than on human selection resulting from humans' destruction of the environment. In the meantime, scientists continue to search for clues about birds' evolution.

ESSENTIAL FACTS

PERIOD TIMELINE					
541–485.4 million years ago (MYA)	485.4–443.8 MYA	443.8–419.2 MYA	419.2–358.9 MYA	358.9–298.9 MYA	298.9–251.9 MYA
CAMBRIAN	ORDOVICIAN	SILURIAN	DEVONIAN	CARBONIFEROUS	PERMIAN

NUMBER OF SPECIES

- As of 2018, the total number of bird species on Earth is more than 10,000.

IMPORTANT ANIMALS AND SPECIMENS

- One of the first birds known to have feathers was *Anchiornis,* which lived in China 160 MYA.
- The first fossil bird to be studied extensively was *Archaeopteryx lithographica,* first found in Germany.
- *Vegavis iaai,* an ancestral cousin of waterfowl, coexisted with nonavian dinosaurs. It was similar to today's ducks and geese.
- *Presbyornis* lived in the Paleogene. It had a beak much like those of today's ducks, which suggests that the duck beak came first and goose beaks evolved later.
- Terror birds were ancient birds that roamed South America between 60 and 2.5 MYA.

	TRIASSIC	JURASSIC	CRETACEOUS	PALEOGENE	NEOGENE	QUATERNARY
		Anchiornis *Archaeopteryx lithographica*	*Vegavis iaai*	*Presbyornis* Terror birds	Terror birds	Terror birds
	251.9–201.3 MYA	201.3–145 MYA	145–66 MYA	66–23 MYA	23–2.6 MYA	2.6 MYA–present

IMPORTANT SCIENTISTS

- Charles Darwin developed his theory of evolution by natural selection in part by studying birds.
- Dr. Evan Saitta and Dr. Jakob Vinther, of the University of Bristol in the United Kingdom, described a single specimen of the ancient bird *Anchiornis* in 2017.
- Kieren Mitchell, of Australia's University of Adelaide, led a DNA study on the evolution of ratites.
- Dr. Jen Bright and Dr. Jesus Marugán-Lobón studied raptor beaks and concluded that their evolution is closely tied to the shape of the head.

QUOTE

"Birds are simply a twig on the dinosaurs' branch of the tree of life."

—*Understanding Evolution* website, University of California, Berkeley

GLOSSARY

archipelago
A group of islands, or a stretch of sea containing many islands.

barb
A part that branches off from a feather's shaft.

bounty
A reward offered by the government for capturing or killing something and turning it in.

clade
A group of species that all descended from a common ancestor.

cladogram
A diagram showing how different species and groups relate to one another.

coevolution
The evolutionary process in which two or more species adapt together, each adapting to the other's changes and affecting the other's evolution.

DNA
Deoxyribonucleic acid, the chemical that is the basis of genetics, through which various traits are passed from parent to child.

insulation
A covering that helps keep a steady internal temperature.

iridescent
Displaying a play of color that occurs when light scatters off the feather's surface and off smooth layers of melanin pigment granules.

lineage
The sequence of descent from an ancestor.

metabolic
Having to do with metabolism, the physical and chemical means by which an organism processes energy.

migration
The seasonal behavior in which a group of animals travels relatively long distances between locations, usually to escape unfavorable conditions or to find food.

molecular
Having to do with molecules, the smallest unit into which a substance can be broken down that is made of two or more atoms and has all of the same properties of the original substance.

natural selection
The major mechanism by which evolution occurs. A trait that offers an advantage for organisms in a population will become more common because those organisms will live longer and produce more offspring.

niche
A species' interaction with its habitat, such as what it feeds on, what feeds on it, and the role it plays in its ecological community.

ornithologist
A scientist who studies birds.

paleontologist
A scientist who studies past life, involving fossils and previous geological periods.

phylogenetic
Having to do with the evolutionary history and development of a group of species or other taxonomic group; illustrated using a phylogenetic tree.

physiology
The physical makeup and bodily processes of an organism.

preen
To groom feathers with a bill.

protein
An amino acid chain present in organic material, such as skin, hair, or blood.

vane
The wide, flat part of a feather.

SELECTED BIBLIOGRAPHY

Duke University. "'Big Bang' of Bird Evolution Mapped: Genes Reveal Deep Histories of Bird Origins, Feathers, Flight and Song." *ScienceDaily*, 11 Dec. 2014, sciencedaily.com. 5 June 2018.

Naish, Darren. "50 Million Years of Incredible Shrinking Theropod Dinosaurs." *Scientific American*, 31 July 2014, blogs.scientificamerican.com. 5 June 2018.

Pepperberg, Irene M. *Alex & Me: How a Scientist and a Parrot Discovered a Hidden World of Animal Intelligence—and Formed a Deep Bond in the Process*. Collins, 2008.

"The Origin of Birds." *Understanding Evolution, University of California Museum of Paleontology*, n.d., evolution.berkeley.edu. 5 June 2018.

FURTHER READINGS

Brusatte, Steve. *The Rise and Fall of the Dinosaurs: A New History of a Lost World*. William Morrow, 2018.

Clark, Robert. *Evolution: A Visual Record*. Phaidon, 2016.

King, David C. *Charles Darwin*. DK, 2007.

ONLINE RESOURCES

To learn more about the evolution of birds, visit **abdobooklinks.com**. These links are routinely monitored and updated to provide the most current information available.

MORE INFORMATION

For more information on this subject, contact or visit the following organizations:

CORNELL LAB OF ORNITHOLOGY

159 Sapsucker Woods Road
Ithaca, NY 14850
800-843-2473
birds.cornell.edu

This organization works to understand birds and other wildlife, involve citizens in scientific discovery, and use scientific knowledge to protect the planet.

NATIONAL AUDUBON SOCIETY

225 Varick Street, Seventh Floor
New York, NY 10014
212-979-3196
audubon.org

This bird conservation organization educates and advocates for protection of birds and their habitats. It does research and maintains bird sanctuaries for exploration and research.

SOURCE NOTES

CHAPTER 1. FROM *T. REX* TO TURKEYS

1. Elizabeth Deatrick. "The Hoatzin: Misfit, Belcher, Genetic Mystery." *Audubon*, 9 Oct. 2015, audubon.org. Accessed 27 July 2018.

2. Joseph Castro. "Archaeopteryx: The Transitional Fossil." *LiveScience*, 14 Mar. 2018, livescience.com. Accessed 27 July 2018.

3. "The Origin of Birds." *Understanding Evolution, University of California Museum of Paleontology*, n.d., evolution.berkeley.edu. Accessed 27 July 2018.

4. Geoffrey Mohan. "When It Comes to DNA, Crocodiles and Birds Flock Together." *Los Angeles Times*, 13 Dec. 2014. www.latimes.com. Accessed 27 July 2018.

5. Frank Gill and David Donsker, eds. "Welcome." *IOC World Bird List Version 8.2*, 25 June 2018, worldbirdnames.org. Accessed 27 July 2018.

CHAPTER 2. FLIGHTLESS BIRDS

1. "Tinamidae: Tinamous." *Encyclopedia of Life*, n.d., eol.org. Accessed 27 July 2018.

2. Alina Bradford. "Ostrich Facts: The World's Largest Bird." *LiveScience*, 17 Sept. 2014, livescience.com. Accessed 27 July 2018.

3. Charles Q. Choi. "Closest Living Relative of Ancient Elephant Bird Is Tiny." *LiveScience*, 22 May 2014, livescience.com. Accessed 27 July 2018.

4. "Flightless Cormorant." *Galapagos Conservation Trust*, 2018, galapagosconservation.org.uk. Accessed 27 July 2018.

5. Allison Fromme. "Why Fly? Flightless Bird Mystery Solved, Say Evolutionary Scientists." *National Geographic*, 13 May 2014, news.nationalgeographic.com. Accessed 27 July 2018.

6. Choi, "Closest Living Relative."

CHAPTER 3. PIGEONS AND DOVES

1. Barry Yeoman. "Why the Passenger Pigeon Went Extinct." *Audubon*, May–June 2014, audubon.org. Accessed 27 July 2018.

2. Chrissie Reilly and Floyd Hertweck. "Cecom History Is for the Birds: Hero Pigeons." *US Army*, 2 Mar. 2012, army.mil. Accessed 27 July 2018.

CHAPTER 4. HUMMINGBIRDS

1. "Giant Hummingbird *Patavona gigas*." *Cornell Lab of Ornithology: Neotropical Birds*, n.d., neotropical.birds.cornell.edu. Accessed 27 July 2018.

2. Adrienne Glick. "*Mellisuga helenae*: Bee Hummingbird." *Animal Diversity Web*, 2002, animaldiversity.org. Accessed 27 July 2018.

3. "Swifts." *Royal Society for the Protection of Birds*, n.d., rspb.org.uk. Accessed 27 July 2018.

4. Molly Michelson. "Hummingbird Evolution." *California Academy of Sciences*, 9 Apr. 2014, calacademy.org. Accessed 27 July 2018.

5. Hannah Osborne. "Hummingbird Evolution: 22-Million-Year-Old Family Tree Shows Rapid Change." *International Business Times*, 3 Apr. 2014. Accessed 27 July 2018.

6. Michelson, "Hummingbird Evolution."

7. "Basic Facts About Hummingbirds." *Defenders of Wildlife*, 2018, defenders.org. Accessed 27 July 2018.

8. Ed Yong. "Hummingbird Evolution Is Booming." *Scientific American*, 3 Apr. 2014, scientificamerican.com. Accessed 27 July 2018.

9. Justin Worland. "This Tiny Hummingbird Can Fly 1,200 Miles Without Stopping." *Time*, 9 Mar. 2016, time.com. Accessed 27 July 2018.

10. "Migration Basics." *Hummingbirds.net*, 2017, hummingbirds.net. Accessed 27 July 2018.

11. "Migration Basics."

12. "Hummingbird Migration." *Hummingbird Central*, 2018, hummingbirdcentral.com. Accessed 27 July 2018.

13. Kathy Piper. "What Do Hummingbirds Eat?" *Bird Watcher's Digest*, March/April 2011, birdwatchersdigest.com. Accessed 27 July 2018.

14. "How to Create a Hummingbird-friendly Yard." *Audubon*, n.d., audubon.org. Accessed 27 July 2018.

15. Bootie Cosgrove-Mather. "Hummingbirds, Flowers, Evolution." *CBS News*, 25 Apr. 2003, cbsnews.com. Accessed 27 July 2018.

CHAPTER 5. TUBENOSES AND PENGUINS

1. Bob Strauss. "30 Basic Bird Groups." *ThoughtCo*, 7 Dec. 2017, thoughtco.com. Accessed 27 July 2018.

2. "Albatrosses." *Seabird Osteology*, 2002–2013, shearwater.nl. Accessed 27 July 2018.

3. John Roach. "Longest Animal Migration Measured, Bird Flies 40,000 Miles a Year." *National Geographic News*, 8 Aug. 2006, news.nationalgeographic.com. Accessed 27 July 2018.

4. Strauss, "30 Basic Bird Groups."

5. "Albatrosses." *National Geographic*, 2018, nationalgeographic.com. Accessed 27 July 2018.

6. Brian Handwerk. "Why Did Penguins Stop Flying? The Answer Is Evolutionary." *National Geographic*, 21 May 2013, nationalgeographic.com. Accessed 27 July 2018.

CHAPTER 6. SHOREBIRDS AND WATERFOWL

1. "Shorebirds 101: What to Look for When You Hit the Water." *Audubon*, n.d., audubon.org. Accessed 27 July 2018.

2. "Fowl-Mouthed Study Finds That Diet Shaped Duck, Goose Beaks." *Brown University*, 30 May 2017, news.brown.edu. Accessed 27 July 2018.

3. "Dasornis Emuinus: Prehistoric Goose Was the Size of a Small Plane and Had Bony Teeth." *Science 2.0*, 26 Sept. 2008, science20.com. Accessed 27 July 2018.

CHAPTER 7. BIRDS OF PREY

1. Richard O. Prum et al. "A Comprehensive Phylogeny of Birds (Aves) Using Targeted Next-Generation DNA Sequencing." *Nature*, vol. 526, 22 Oct. 2015. pp. 569–573. Accessed 27 July 2018.

2. Niki Wilson. "The Reign of the Terror Birds." *BBC*, 24 July 2015, bbc.com. Accessed 27 July 2018.

3. Sean Markey. "Largest 'Terror Bird' Fossil Found in Argentina." *National Geographic News*, 25 Oct. 2006, news.nationalgeographic.com. Accessed 27 July 2018.

4. Wilson, "The Reign of the Terror Birds."

5. "Which Bird Is the Fastest Runner?" *Audubon*, Sept. 2017, audubon.org. Accessed 27 July 2018.

6. "Adaptive Radiation: Darwin's Finches." *PBS: Evolution Library*, 2001, pbs.org. Accessed 27 July 2018.

7. Meghan Bartels. "Proof of Evolution? Birds of Prey Avoid Extinction by Growing Longer Beaks in Just 10 Years." *Newsweek*, 28 Nov. 2017, newsweek.com. Accessed 27 July 2018.

8. "Birds of Prey Constrained in the Beak Evolution Race." *Phys.org*, 26 Apr. 2016, phys.org. Accessed 27 July 2018.

9. Jen A. Bright et al. "The Shapes of Bird Beaks Are Highly Controlled by Nondietary Factors." *Proceedings of the National Academy of Sciences*, vol. 113, no. 19, 10 May 2016. pp. 5352–5357. Accessed 27 July 2018.

10. Jeremy Plester. "Weatherwatch: Tawny Owls Get Tawnier." *Guardian*, 24 Aug. 2014, theguardian.com. Accessed 27 July 2018.

CHAPTER 8. PARROTS AND KIN

1. "Parrots." *National Geographic*, 2018, nationalgeographic.com. Accessed 27 July 2018.

2. "Parrots."

3. Betty Jean Craige. "Craige: How African Greys Have Evolved." *Athens Banner-Herald*, 15 Dec. 2012, onlineathens.com. Accessed 27 July 2018.

4. "Kea." *New Zealand Birds Online*, 2013, nzbirdsonline.org.nz. Accessed 27 July 2018.

5. Dinitia Smith. "A Thinking Bird or Just Another Birdbrain?" *New York Times*, 9 Oct. 1999, nytimes.com. Accessed 27 July 2018.

6. Timothy F. Wright et al. "A Multilocus Molecular Phylogeny of the Parrots (Psittaciformes): Support for a Gondwanan Origin During the Cretaceous." *Molecular Biology and Evolution*, vol. 25, no. 10, 1 Oct. 2008. pp. 2141–2156. Accessed 27 July 2018.

7. Nick Sly. "Parrot Bio-Geography and Evolution." *10,000 Birds*, 2012, 10000birds.com. Accessed 27 July 2018.

8. José L. Tella and Fernando Hiraldo. "Illegal and Legal Parrot Trade Shows a Long-Term, Cross-Cultural Preference for the Most Attractive Species Increasing Their Risk of Extinction." *PLoS One*, vol. 9 no. 9, 16 Sept. 2014. Accessed 27 July 2018.

CHAPTER 9. PERCHING BIRDS

1. "Passerines: Perching Birds." *Myriad Editions*, n.d., assets.press.princeton.edu. Accessed 27 July 2018.

2. Scott V. Edwards and John Harshman. "Passeriformes. Perching Birds, Passerine Birds." *Tree of Life Web Project*, 6 Feb. 2013, tolweb.org. Accessed 27 July 2018.

3. "Passerines: Perching Birds."

4. Ian Sample. "Sprouting Feathers and Lost Teeth: Scientists Map the Evolution of Birds." *Guardian*, 11 Dec. 2014, theguardian.com. Accessed 27 July 2018.

5. Haruka Wada. "The Development of Birdsong." *Nature Education Knowledge*, vol. 3 no. 10, 2010. Accessed 27 July 2018.

6. Shaena Montanari. "We Knew Ravens Are Smart. But Not This Smart." *National Geographic*, 13 July 2017, news.nationalgeographic.com. Accessed 27 July 2018

CHAPTER 10. PRESENT-DAY RESEARCH

1. Helen Briggs. "Baby Bird Fossil Is 'Rarest of the Rare.'" *BBC News*, 5 Mar. 2018, bbc.com. Accessed 27 July 2018.

2. Duke University. "'Big Bang' of Bird Evolution Mapped: Genes Reveal Deep Histories of Bird Origins, Feathers, Flight and Song." *ScienceDaily*, 11 Dec. 2014, sciencedaily.com. Accessed 27 July 2018.

3. Duke University, "'Big Bang' of Bird Evolution Mapped."

4. Duke University, "'Big Bang' of Bird Evolution Mapped."

5. Duke University, "'Big Bang' of Bird Evolution Mapped."

6. "The Earth's Sixth Mass Extinction?" *Understanding Evolution, University of California Museum of Paleontology*, n.d., evolution.berkeley.edu. Accessed 27 July 2018.

INDEX

ABOUT THE AUTHOR

Carol Hand has a PhD in zoology from the University of Georgia. She has taught college biology, written biology assessments for national assessment companies, and written high school science curricula for a national company. For the past nine years, she has been a freelance science writer. She has authored more than 50 young-adult science books, including biology titles such as *Introduction to Genetics, Reviving Extinct Species, Bringing Back Our Oceans,* and *Climate Change: Our Warming Earth.*